D1267670

On Becoming A

HEALTH AND
HUMAN SERVICES
MANAGER

On Becoming A

HEALTH AND
HUMAN SERVICES
MANAGER

A Practical Guide
For Clinicians and Counselors

Paul G. Quinnett

Foreword by William Van Ornum

CONTINUUM | NEW YORK

1989

The Continuum Publishing Company
370 Lexington Avenue
New York, NY 10017

Printed in the United States of America

Library of Congress Cataloging-in-Publication Data

Quinnett, Paul G., 1939–
    On becoming a health and human services manager : a practical
guide for clinicians and counselors / Paul G. Quinnett ; foreword by
William Van Ornum.
        p.   cm. — (Continuum counseling series)
    Bibliography: p.
    ISBN 0-8264-0508-8
    1. Health services administration. I. Title. II. Series.
    [DNLM: 1. Health Facility Administrators. 2. Health Services–
–organization & administration. W 84.1 Q7o]
RA393.Q85   1989
362.1'068—dc20
DNLM/DLC
for Library of Congress   89-7332
                                                                  CIP

To Mary Higgins and Beanie.
Remember the good times.

Contents

Foreword

On Becoming a Health and Human Services Manager by Paul Quinnett is the newest volume in The Continuum Counseling Series.

The Continuum Counseling Series presents practical guides for everyone interested in each book's topic or in learning about counseling. And it brings to readers authors with proven counseling experience as well as a knowledge of current research and approaches to their topic.

Many counselors avoid books in their field because many titles on counseling are either highly technical or are edited collections of papers. Books in the Continuum Counseling Series develop the entire subject in a unified way and are written by a single author (or team of coauthors who work closely together) and the entire series is designed so that the books complement and reinforce each other.

Many professional associations have endorsed the idea that books on counseling and therapy should be readable and practical. The American Psychiatric Association sponsors a number of trade books, written for psychiatrists but done in a way that they are of interest to the general public; and the American Psychological Association, while continuing to emphasize the scientific aspects of psychology, now also values practical volumes of "giving psychology away."

We hope books in The Continuum Counseling Series will be helpful not only to general readers, but to professors and students in fields such as psychology, social work, psychiatry,

9

guidance and counseling, and nursing, and all counselors and psychotherapists—in short, helpers of every kind.

Despite many conflicting claims about counseling, the research is almost unanimous that empathy and understanding are essential in any effective counseling. Each book in the Continuum Counseling Series is designed to help readers become more empathic to individuals struggling with issues related to the topic of the volume. *On Becoming a Health and Human Services Manager* by Dr. Paul G. Quinnett is an essential management guide written specifically for those in the helping professions—from mental health to nursing to teaching to social work—and many more.

Paul Quinnett's body of work doesn't need an introduction, but it is flattering to be part of any endeavor of which he is a part. His first book, *The Troubled People Book* (New York: Continuum, 1985), has guided many individuals toward the therapeutic help they need. The American Library Association's *Booklist* praised it as "without doubt, one of the most honest, reassuring, nonpaternalistic, and useful 'self-help' books ever to appear." His best-selling *Suicide: The Forever Decision* (New York: Continuum, 1988) is a heart-to-heart talk between a master therapist and anyone considering this drastic and life-ending decision. I suspect that book has had affirming effects on many lives, on individuals who will not proclaim this assistance in public but who will carry with them profound thanks to Paul Quinnett. Dr. Quinnett has established his reputation as a wise clinician and superb writer; now he helps all of us in the helping professions who have ever had to manage others or be in positions of clinical leadership. I read *On Becoming a Health and Human Services Manager* eagerly; wished I could have absorbed it years ago, and now enthusiastically welcome its inclusion into The Continuum Counseling Series.

Working in clinical leadership is a commitment, not just a job, and Quinnett proclaims "If this work wasn't noble, I wouldn't do it." He recognizes that the power and influence that come with positions of authority can be enjoyed; but they must be used properly, to help clients, staff, and organization.

In the past decade there has been an influx of books on management, many of these written in a popular style for the general reader. Most of these are aimed toward the business manager. Now we have an authoritative, specific, and helpful book for everyone who works at managing therapists, educators, and other workers in the human services field.

All of Paul Quinnett's books share the "ring of authenticity," the authority of someone who has discovered, put into practice his own insights, and validated the rich body of knowledge of others in the field. This new book brims with wisdom. Quinnett points out how 20 percent of a system can cause 80 percent of the problems: focus on the 20 percent. As manager you will be exhorted to expect staff to "deliver the goods." Ways of getting into control of paperwork (bane of many clinicians) are given. To monitor your control of paperwork, put a dot on a piece of paper every time you read it. After a week, you are in trouble if there is lots of paper on your desk with lots of dots.

Interpersonal issues take up much of any manager's time. Dr. Quinnett advises how to handle some very delicate issues with fairness and humanity, and for those in a leadership position to "forego love and settle for respect." We have an image of Quinnett-as-leader rolling up his sleeves and pitching in: "I will never ask them to do something for which they are not qualified, or that is unethical, or that I would not do myself."

Good management and good clinical work aren't mutually exclusive. For any person who was drawn to the helping professions out of an interest in others or of putting some ideals into practice, this book will show ways to involve others in putting the mission into practice. Paul Quinnett encourages all leaders to bring their organizations back into focus with their ideals, and to enjoy this noble goal. "A dream with big rolling wheels is empowering." This book can help you to become an effective leader in your chosen profession.

William Van Ornum, Ph.D.
Marist College
Poughkeepsie, New York

General Editor
The Continuum Counseling Series

Introduction

Because I know you're busy, I'm going to keep this introduction short. Because I'm busy too, I'm going to keep this whole book short.

This work grew out of a request for me to lead a workshop for midmanagers in a statewide mental health system. Having been to only a few management seminars over the years I was, like most clinicians, academically unprepared to manage others—let alone teach the subject.

But the more I prepared for the workshop, the more I realized that what I had learned and read and absorbed over the twenty years I have been a manager was not insubstantial. Then I remembered my secretary's comment as she handed me the inch-thick set of notes I had dictated for my presentation, "Is this your next book?"

I guess it was.

Whatever else this book is, it is intended to be manager friendly, easy to read and, I hope, useful, practical and occasionally enjoyable. But most of all it is intended to introduce the reader to this business of managing others for the welfare of those we serve.

This book is not a shorthand approach to personnel management and the legal requirements of employers. For example, I do not attempt to cover such public policies as the Fair Labor Standards Act, issues of sexual harassment, nondiscrimination or affirmative action. Based primarily on personal experience and my own nondirected reading program, I have not attempted to replace more formal texts on the theory, research, and practice of management, although I have listed some of these in the appendix.

Rather, my intention here is to try to meet exactly those needs expressed by managers when they are asked, "To do your job better, what do you most need to learn about management?" Long on practicalities, this book was planned, organized, and written in response to the results of just such a survey.

So that you'll know my perspective here, I've spent my professional career in the field of mental health, both in the public and private sectors. Therefore, the language of this book reflects this background, although I hope that what I have to say will be useful to anyone working in the broad field of health and human services.

Over the years I've supervised (at least administratively, and clinically where appropriate to my own training) nurses, psychiatrists, general practice physicians, psychologists, social workers, alcohol and drug treatment specialists, pastoral counselors, occupational therapists, recreational therapists, marriage and family therapists, geriatric specialists, case managers, developmental disabilities specialists, general office staff, paraprofessionals, students of every stripe and volunteers. (If I've missed someone, I apologize.)

I especially wrote this book for one person: the counselor or clinician (be he or she psychologist, psychiatrist, nurse, social worker, pastor, etc.) who is, in small part or large, responsible for the work of other people. Especially I wrote it for the person just entering the role of manager—the beginner, the novice, the recently promoted.

If you're still getting over the shock of being a boss, welcome to the club. If you've been around awhile, maybe you will find a few things in here that will make managing others easier and, hopefully, more fun. Chief executive officers probably won't learn much from reading this book, but they might find it useful as a short course for the people they are planning to promote.

Lastly, I wrote this book for the clients or patients or whatever you might call the people-in-need in the system in which you work. People-helping staff (and the services they deliver) are our only meaningful resource; manage them poorly and the people we hope to serve get less of what it is we have to offer— manage them well and everyone benefits.

Paul Quinnett, 1989

Author's Note

In deference to both sexes and to avoid the "he/she" awk-
wardness of recent invention, I have alternated the gender
pronoun throughout the text of this book. Not only does this
turn taking reflect the new reality of women in management,
but it relieves both reader and author the distraction such an
artifice demands.

On Becoming A

HEALTH AND
HUMAN SERVICES
MANAGER

1

The Promotion

To my knowledge, no one becomes a manager in the human service field except by coming up through the ranks. Everyone is required to earn one's spurs, first as a counselor or clinician, then as a manager. Psychiatrists and other physicians, partly because you have to pay them so much, may start their careers in the private or public sector with a fancy title, but as managers of others they know about as much as the rest of us—which, since you have some apparent need to read this book, you will agree is practically zero.

We all start from the same place: perfect ignorance contaminated only by our prejudices, personal experience, and, maybe unfortunately, some preconceived notions about what makes people tick. Fear and trembling about managing others badly is part of the job too, but of course that happens every time we do something for the first time—including accepting a promotion to additional responsibility and authority.

Here is my first question: Is it a help or a hindrance for the manager of others to be a trained people helper?

I don't know if I know the answer myself, but I do know that until you, as an employee of a system, come to some kind of understanding about the role you have been asked to fulfill, you will remain at least perplexed, at worst agonized.

I will, in the chapter entitled "An Inward Look," at least explore this question of our personal life experiences and training and whether we are, in some ways, handicapped to become good managers. But for now, it has been my experience that at

21

least a few managers never do figure out what it was they agreed to when they were promoted, had no idea what they had gotten themselves into by accepting a promotion and, as a result, managed their staffs poorly, managed themselves poorly, and gave their bosses no end of grief.

These unhappy people were plagued by uncertainty about what they were doing. They muddled along with no sense of accomplishment, no sense of well-being, and no sense of satisfaction with getting the job done well. A few of them became tyrants to their staff, a few of them divided their loyalties wrongly and were fired, and a few just got fed up, burned out, and left the field.

Mind you, these were good people. Someone had seen fit to promote them to a position of responsibility. They were up-and-comers. They were, if you take the long view, what the health care system needed—bright, capable, energetic people who might be counted on to be the leaders of tomorrow.

But something went wrong. Never having managed others before, they were suddenly on unfamiliar ground. They made mistakes.

Unwittingly, they upset their supervisees. Not knowing better, they disappointed their supervisors. After living through their first serious management crisis, they discovered they were no longer one of the gang, but were part of the hateful "they" of administration—the same hateful "they" they had, themselves, once loved to complain about.

And yet seeking support from above seemed a bit alien, like taking one's knives to the Philistines to have them sharpened.

Innocent in the beginning, they discovered hidden costs to the job of manager—painful little obligations they didn't know were in the package when they signed on. Like firing someone who had been a friend and coworker.

Without the same level of support by colleagues, and no longer certain as to who could be trusted with a confidence or with whom one could share the weight of the new burden, these managers began to realize what the phrase "It's lonely at the top" meant. And they didn't like it much.

Worse, they didn't have the skills or the tools necessary to do the job they were asked to do. The big paycheck that was to offset the loss of being a line staffer didn't do it and, when they reflected on what had happened and why, they remembered one of their basic lessons in human values: money never compensates for lost relationships.

And so they left; some in anger, some disillusioned, some with a boot print on their backsides.

And some stay on. Even now. They may have a drawer full of antacids, or they may have gone over to the security that comes from hiding out in one's job by doing nothing innovative, saying nothing controversial, and accomplishing only enough to avoid being sacked. You may even know such a manager.

But my operating assumption for the reader of this book is that you neither want to leave the field prematurely, become a stress case, or gradually turn into one of the bureaucratic do-nothings. And my hope is that your management job can be a rewarding one, even fun and invigorating.

Management doesn't *have* to be miserable—more, it shouldn't be. With a little work, some new skills and a new perspective or two, you can become a good manager, maybe an excellent one. Best of all, the clients your system serves will be the real benefactors of your promotion and new job—which is probably why you got into this line of work in the first place.

In the interest of keeping things brief, I only want to say one more thing.

If you are honest with yourself about why you agreed to accept a promotion to become a manager, I think you will find your motives are no different than those of people who become managers in any other system of business or government. An honest look in the mirror should tell you that you became a manager for a handful of fairly simple reasons: more money, more prestige, and more power.

Money and prestige are neither a sin nor a crime in America and you, even as an original people helper, have every right to strive for them. But power?

Yes. Despite the average human service worker's low opinion of power and those who seek it, it is my view that unless you want power, you will not be a good manager. You have to, I think, come to understand and accept your needs for power and control and to influence others. Without this self-awareness you run the risk of not knowing why you do what you do, or for what purposes.

Managers should want power; not to build heartless, mean-spirited empires that ravage the innocent and the helpless, but good power to achieve good ends. Without power, how will you (or anyone) bring about the political and social changes necessary to build the kind of care systems our clients need? Without the power to influence your staff and the CEO or board above you, how will you reach the highest standards of care possible for your clients, community, or hospital? Without power and your willingness to use it, how will you get the job done they have asked you to do?

Power is to change what action is to ideas; without it, there is only so much smoke and rhetoric. Unless you want to be seen as only so much smoke and rhetoric, I'd suggest you step up to the concept of power and shake hands.

It is, in my view, absolutely necessary that someone accept power and put it to good ends. And while your motives to be a manager may "appear" less noble than those of the therapist or nurse or counselor you started out to be, I fear you will make a grave mistake if you do not expand your vision and see your new job as every bit as acceptable, important, virtuous, and meaningful as those of the people who work for you. Maybe more so!

There is no evil in power, only in those who wield it.

(Note: Some people doodle aimlessly in meetings; I scribble. What I scribble are epigrams, one-liners, and other mostly futile efforts to boil out the essence of whatever subject matter we happen to be discussing in one director's meeting or another. I have indulged myself in this dubious practice for at least two decades and will, therefore, apologize right now for this epigram and any others that slip from my pen throughout this text—provided the editor doesn't whack them out altogether.)

Finally, someone once asked me why I stayed so long in middle management in a public-sector mental-health center when I could have gone into full-time private practice and made those so-called big bucks. I popped off the following answer without thinking, "For the power and influence, of course."

Later, thinking over this unseemly remark, I realized it was true. Except for the dear friends and colleagues with whom I have enjoyed working these many years, I have remained a manager throughout my career because it was the only place I had enough power to positively influence the lives of so many more people than I might have been able to help all by myself. I don't apologize for this attitude, nor do I think anyone similarly placed should.

Drafting policies, serving on committees, helping change laws, training others, supervising people to grow and achieve, fighting the good fight with my colleagues against our common foes, working out all the knotty little problems that hector an agency, a community, a care system, and the people it tries to serve—that is what it has all been about for me. And it has been a good twenty-five years.

Maybe it will be that way for you, too. I hope so.

Oh, and before I forget (and even if this is a belated one),

Congratulations on your promotion!

2

The Job

Among the duties listed in your job description as a supervisor, coordinator, director, or whatever, you should find (usually at the very bottom) a phrase that reads roughly as follows: "And all other assigned duties." These "other" duties are what I want to talk about in this chapter.

If you read over the major responsibilities in your job description, you already know what administration expects from you in broad terms: to hire people, develop programs, supervise, coordinate, direct, and, in general, see to it that the goals you help set for your service area are met. You knew this going in.

What you maybe didn't know was that there are a lot of unspoken responsibilities tucked away in any management job title. For example, is a manager's job simply to supervise and organize the work of those below him? For many years I thought that is what being a manager meant. I was wrong.

If a manager is only responsible to the people below him, he is a foreman, or a skilled technician who leads a team of other technicians, or a supervisor of a small cog of people in the organization whose input to the organization as a whole is neither needed nor wanted—but he is not a manager.

A manager is responsible for a great deal more than just the work of those below him. In many ways, a manager is responsible for the health and welfare of his *entire* organization. It is not enough to take care of just his department and "his people." To be a manager, his allegiance, ideas, efforts, and commitment

26

must be to work for the benefit of the agency or institution for whom he works. This view and acceptance of responsibilities is what separates the true managers from those who are only paid manager's wages.

The unspoken responsibilities I will now describe, since they have to do with role and function rather than duties per se, may be more important than anything specifically written into your job description. Based on years of managing people helpers, these ten thoughts are in no order of importance—except for the first one.

The Manager Is Responsible

1. To Make the Boss Look Good   Once you've stepped out of the ranks of the line staff and moved to a position of authority, you have a different set of obligations to your new boss, one of which is to make him or her look good. (Note: I don't like the term "line" staff vs. some other kind of staff. However, since the days of Julius Caesar, the troops who went into battle first have been called "the line" and the habit seems a hard one to break.)

Some wag once said that the boss may not always be right, but she is *always* the boss. And while there is a little message of fear in this one-liner, it is very much the case that the person you report to can only be effective to the degree her immediate supervisory staff (you) support her leadership.

To be supportive doesn't mean you have become a lap dog and agree with everything the boss says and does, but it does mean you have to get behind a decision or new policy and let your own staff know, by word and deed, that you support the action—sometimes even when you privately think the idea isn't such a good one. (I trust you realize the remote possibility that your judgment in all matters could, at least once in a great while, be slightly off the mark.)

Failure to support the boss can lead, rather immediately, to the following: staff unrest because they are being asked to do something impossible or irresponsible, a breach in the confidence between the staff and administration and, as a result, poor morale, lower productivity, and, in the end, poorer service to clients.

The worst consequence of not supporting the boss is the development of the "we-they" split; we being the staff, they being the administration—of which, by the way, you are now a part. If you are not very careful in how you handle a developing split of this kind, you may find yourself looking for another job.

If you strongly disagree with your boss about some decision or other, you owe it to her to tell her the whys and wherefores, in detail and as clearly as you can. But only in the privacy of her office. Though she may not always accept or, for that matter, even like your input, she still needs your counsel, information, and opinion. Never, I say, NEVER, take a public or in-front-of staff position diametrically opposed to something you know your boss is heavily committed to. This can make your boss look bad. And if she *looks* bad, she may make you *feel* bad. There is a line from Shakespeare that covers this situation rather nicely, "Never strike a king unless you can kill him."

A boss who is made to look good by her subordinates is a happy boss. Happy bosses are even more happy when their bosses are happy because the job they have given her is being done well. It is easy to forget that directors and CEOs have bosses, but they do. And despite how self-confident they may appear to you, they are no different than the rest of us in the wanting-to-look-good department.

Finally, since your responsibilities include helping to get the job done well, you have a great deal of power to make your boss look good, not only to your staff, but to her boss as well. It should be obvious that working for a happy boss is much better than working for an unhappy one.

2. To Get the Mission Accomplished If your agency or institution doesn't have one, you need a mission statement. The mission statement is the answer to the question, "What is our business?" It doesn't have to be long, complicated, or burdened down with great social implications or high-toned observations on the nature of man. It only has to say what the heck everyone who comes to work every morning is trying to get done while they are there all day.

It might read: Our mission is to serve our clients with all the resources available to us so as to maximize the mental and physical health of those people in our community who are most in need.

It could say anything. In some ways it doesn't matter much what the exact statement says, just so long as the leadership gave the mission statement some studied thought and are able to communicate to the entire staff what it means. I call the mission statement the little white ball, as in golf.

One of the best examples of the little white ball is the mission statement of the American Telephone and Telegraph company: "Our business is to serve people." Sounds simple and most of us know it by heart. But from this early statement of the mission of AT&T, the greatest service monopoly in history grew. Its standards of service, research and development, technological advances, advertising, marketing . . . , everything this huge organization set out to accomplish was in the service of its customers. And until the monopoly was dismantled in recent years, it succeeded like no other.

To hit a golf ball you have to keep your eye on it. To hit it well, you have to keep your eye on it all the time—through the swing, the hit, and the first part of the follow through. If you take your eye off the ball, even for a split second, you will produce a slice or a hook or, in my case, you may miss the little white thing all together. The same thing happens in agencies and institutions.

People helpers sometimes take their eye off the ball. The result can be an inordinate amount of time and energy going into solving staff problems rather than solving client problems. Sometimes you will see agencies riding off in all directions at once, chasing new ventures totally at odds with the original mission statement. Uncertain of what business they are truly about, an agency without a clear, up-to-date mission statement can become a huge mess just waiting to happen.

In my view the single greatest cause for confusion, mismanagement, turnover, and the eventual collapse of a service agency is that someone (usually the CEO or his board, or both) took his eye off the ball.

(As an aside, I might note that if you don't have a mission statement and decide to sit down with your management team and think one up, be prepared for conflict. For all the reasons managers believe strongly about the importance of their work, they feel strongly about why they do what they do. Seldom, if ever, do different managers from different departments of the same agency share exactly the same reasons for the why of the organization. The result of these unspoken differences of opinion, once you begin discussions about a mission statement, will be obvious in a matter of minutes.)

Your job as a manager will be much easier if you know the mission statement of your agency by heart and can keep your eye on the ball. If fact, I'd suggest that about once a week you take a moment to ask yourself the following question: "How are we hitting the ball today?"

3. *To Keep and Maintain Good Morale*   If you're going to make your boss look good (by getting your job done well), you will need some happy troops, or at least relatively happy ones. Keeping morale high may be one of the most important jobs they forgot to list on your job description.

Why? Because low morale leads to absenteeism, turnover, lowered productivity, poor patient care, and, therefore, the failure of the agency to accomplish its mission.

Some studies indicate that about 10 percent of the work force is chronically disgruntled and that nothing and no one can make them happy about the fact that they have to work for a living. As I see it you can do two things with an employee who suffers from chronic distemper: help the staff learn to laugh about it (as Grumpy's coworkers did in *Snow White and the Seven Dwarfs*) or, figure out how to help him change.

If the staff can't learn to laugh with a chronically unhappy or angry coworker and, as a result, morale is lowered by this person's presence (including your own morale), then something has to be done and it is your job to take action. (How to counsel and, if necessary, discipline or terminate an employee will be covered in the chapter on firing.)

Complaints of broken air-conditioners, people smoking in the wrong places, salaries that are too low, insufficient parking, you name it, staff will complain about it. And that's okay. Without someone complaining once in a while it is easy to overlook things that need fixing. But serious signs of slipping morale need to be identified, investigated, and acted upon—otherwise, the mission of the agency is jeopardized.

4. To Advocate for Clients   If you take client welfare as the bottom line for the existence of human service agencies (why else have them?), then it follows that a manager's job includes taking an advocacy role toward the clients her agency serves. This may mean developing new programs, studying the latest treatment methods available, fighting for more staff to do the job, taking strong positions with funding sources for more money and fewer needless regulations, getting involved in political actions to move legislation that will benefit clients, and, in dozens of other ways, putting in the time and energy to move society forward into a more humane world.

Managers, because of their positions and titles, have power to influence—a lot more power than most of them realize. When they fail to use that power to make things happen for the clients their agencies serve, to me, at least, they are not fulfilling all the requirements of the job.

It helps me to remember that for those of us in the people-helping field, the good fight is always there to fight, always needs fighting, and, maybe more than anything else, gives a clear meaning to the why of human service work.

5. To Work on Yourself   The job of manager is more than the sum of its title and salary; possibly a great deal more. To know what a manager is, and can be, requires the manager to work on himself. There is nothing automatic about power—someone may give it to you, but you must learn to use it well enough so that it will bring you respect. To learn to use your position well, you must study, read, attend what training in management you can, ask questions, seek advice from older hands, and otherwise undertake a growth-oriented personal development program.

If it turns out being a supervisor is making you miserable or sick (ulcers, migraine, anxiety, etc.) then you owe it to yourself, your staff, your boss, and, finally, the clients you serve, to get yourself into therapy to learn what is happening and what you can do about it. Having worked with many people-helper supervisors over the years in my private practice, I can assure you that your problems around managing others are neither new nor particularly difficult to resolve. Personally, I think support groups for managers are a good idea and, if you don't have one in your area, you might consider starting one.

6. To Minimize Absenteeism and Turnover Absenteeism and turnover may be part of an overall poor morale problem or, in some cases, part of an institution's norms. I've heard managers say, "Ah, people don't stick around here very long. A year or two, and then they move on to greener pastures. You know how it is."

A manager with this kind of attitude either doesn't understand the high cost of turnover or, because of this attitude, is part of the reason people don't stick around. While Americans are a highly mobile work force (absolutely nomadic by European and Japanese standards) and feel they have an inalienable right to change jobs whenever the mood strikes them (and professional people helpers maybe more so), turnover still has a very negative impact on a social service or treatment agency. Caseloads must be transferred, therapeutic relationships must be severed, new employee start-up expenses are high in terms of training and orientation and, at least for many long-term clients, the atmosphere of constant change in staff does nothing to give them a feeling of stability or, for that matter, a sense of lasting commitment from one human being to another.

Absenteeism can also become institutionalized. I was once about to hire a man for a job as an outpatient therapist. He was going to join our staff from a much larger state institution and, knowing he had to give them notice of his intention to leave, I asked him how much time he needed. He replied (apparently thinking out loud) that since he had twenty days of unused sick leave, he would need about a month before he could sign on with us.

"Are you planning to be sick?" I asked.

His neck flushed and he stammered, "Uh . . . no, I just don't want to lose my sick days."

Since I didn't want to take him to raise, I didn't hire him.

Because the mission statement usually implies using resources efficiently, effectively, and economically to serve the people, it becomes the manager's job not to waste these, or allow them to be wasted. Since the resources (the staff) must be managed to maximize the hours of service available for clients, part of a manager's job is to try to learn the reasons for turnover and absenteeism and then, once the cause is understood, to try to do something about it. People leave jobs for many reasons and it is, at the very least, the manager's job not to be one of those reasons.

7. *To Communicate* Communication is such an overused word I even have trouble saying it these days but, because the successful manager must be a successful communicator, I feel obliged to communicate this communication to you. (Enough communication?)

If you draw a series of those arrows pointing to and from you (the arrows of communication), you will quickly see that your job involves not only talking with the people you supervise, but also communicating with your boss.

The people below you count on you to be a representative of their views, concerns, worries, and, when asked specifically, to get them answers to their questions. If you fail to carry their views forward with clarity, staff will lose confidence in your ability to represent them and, as sometimes happens, they may decide to go around you—with a memo to your boss, by forming some sort of action committee, or by talking with union representatives.

One of the worst things that can happen to a supervisor is to have one or more of his staff go "over his head." This is a clear vote of no confidence and, unless you are able to pull some pretty clever tricks out of the hat, you may soon find your job intolerable.

The reason many people do not carry the staff's concerns upstairs is that their boss doesn't like to hear about grumbling down in the ranks. (Despite the continuing evolution of the species, the practice of killing the messenger who brings the bad news didn't end in Roman times.) But bringing bad news to the boss *is* your job. There is no way around it. Your boss is counting on you for information, even information he might not like. He needs to know when staff are upset, why they are upset, and what you can recommend be done about it. Believe me, your boss won't look good if your department files a complaint (en masse) with *his* boss. (Remember point one: make the boss look good.)

Please note: In my experience much of the "bad news" supervisors carry to their boss could have been avoided if, and only if, the supervisor had had the fortitude to say the word *no*. As a manager you should know company policy, procedures, benefits, and how change is going to take place. You should know the answers to almost all the questions that might come up. If you do your job and know the game plan as well as your boss, only rarely should you have to take questions and concerns of staff to a higher level. The good manager only takes problems to the boss that he does not have the knowledge or the authority to solve—everything else should have already been handled.

A manager communicates up and down, but she also communicates sideways. The sideways communication is equally important to getting the mission of the agency accomplished. Without good communication across program lines, in jointly staffed committees, between agencies and institutions, the entire service system suffers and, in the bargain, the clients it is designed to serve suffer as well.

I have seen many otherwise promising managers take the position that "It's us against them!" with respect to other programs within the agency or between their agency and another. Or they will assume the kind of ethnocentric attitude that says, "We're the best and everyone else in our field is a drooling cretin!"

These primitive tribal attitudes may have some value on the Little League ball field, but they have no place in social service or mental health work and, especially, in the makeup of a manager. Skillful diplomacy is critical to the mission of helping troubled people through our systems and I, for one, am always sickened by how much valuable time and money is wasted on turf wars sponsored, in large part, by mean little people with mean little attitudes.

(If your job descriptions for managers do not include a requirement to be a good communicator, you might consider changing them.)

8. *To Anticipate Problems and Knock Them Down Early*
Training in human service and for most people helpers teaches
us, generally, to sit back and wait for clients with problems to
come to us for wise advice or therapy to fix the problem. To
take this position (that all the important problems will eventually be delivered to your office) is, in my opinion, precisely
the wrong position for a manager to take. It is like saying,
"When things out there get bad enough, people will come to me
for help."

Question: Unless you enjoy riding to the rescue or cleaning
up messes, why wait?

One of the reasons social workers tend to make good managers is that, compared to some of the rest of us, they are more
familiar with the concept of outreach—the idea that if you go
and find the problem before it requires drastic solutions, you
can save the client and his family a lot of expense and grief. If
you, as a manager, apply this outreach concept to managing
people helpers you will, I think, find a similar benefit.

For example, suppose you hear though the grapevine that
one of your staff is having trouble at home and has had to leave
work early a couple of times to take care of her children
because her husband has moved out. Do you wait until her
absenteeism becomes excessive, or do you wander down to her
office and offer a bit of sympathy and maybe some help by way
of administrative relief? Knowing you have an audit scheduled
in two months, do you wait until you've a week to prepare, or
do you get started early and have everything shipshape well
before the order comes to get ready for the guys in the green
eyeshades?

In my experience the smartest managers can see, like mete-
orologists, dark clouds forming over some far horizon long
before someone has to shout, "Get inside! It's raining cats and
dogs!" A manager who comes to me and tells me how he saw
this problem brewing, how he checked it out, and what he did
to gently avert some disaster or other is a manager I can hug!
And if I get the chance, I'll promote him.

9. *To Teach* If you toss out the idea that people have learned
all the "important things" by the time they graduate from what-

ever final training they've received, you're off to a good start as a manager. Adults of *any* age are capable of learning and to a great degree the job of the manager is to teach these adult learners things they don't know. Oh, they may think they know everything because, after all, they have MDs and PhD's and MSWs and RNs and such after their names, but after you've been a manager for a few months, you may suddenly sit up straight in the middle of the night and say to yourself, "Gee! About some pretty basic things, these people are really stupid!" I know I have.

Granted your staff are not eighteen-year-old high-school dropouts and, yes, some of them have had more education than entire cities in the sixteenth century, but that does not mean they still don't have a few things to learn about; procedures, policies, hiring practices, why the agency is doing this or that, what's happening with funding sources, politics, how to get along with each other, and a hundred other administrative or regulatory changes that may be coming and may (read: usually do) affect their work.

Formal classroom teaching may also be required. Leading seminars, lecturing, organizing study groups are skills a manager should begin to develop if he doesn't have them.

Finally, because professional people-helper staff already know just about all there is to know about everything and will rarely take a direct order without questioning it, a manager must learn how to teach, educate, cajole, process, and persuade such people to go along with any new program. This is tough, draining work. A fellow manager of mine spoke to this issue after a long week of trying to get her staff to do something new and different. "Why can't we just knock 'em out? You know, give 'em a good right cross and knock 'em out?"

10. To Facilitate Change   For almost ten years I have kept an epigram (a 1983 slip of the pen) tacked to the cork board above my desk. It reads: "The only thing worse than change, is sudden change." And right next to this reminder, I keep another epigram that also came to me at the end of a hard day of problem solving, "If this work wasn't noble, I wouldn't do it."

Because formal people-helping groups (the churches notwithstanding) only evolved into recognizable institutions within the last half of the twentieth century, I try to remind myself that compared to the other institutions upon which we rely for our care, cures, and comforts (government, universities, churches, the medical profession) we in the mental health or social service business do not enjoy the flywheels of historical habits, traditions, customs, and practices that enable older institutions to function more or less smoothly. No, in order to keep our institutions moving along from month to month without falling apart before our very eyes, we must invent a new kind of wheel at least a couple of times a week.

If you stand way back from the people-helping movement and scan forward from the post–World War II years to the present, I think you will be dizzied by both the velocity and absolute volume of change our field has undergone.

From the child guidance and family-counseling clinics of the 1940s and 50s, to the years of deinstitutionalization of our state hospitals, to the federal Mental Health Act of 1963 and its later demise, to the rise of the independent practice of psychology, social work, nursing, and counselors of every sort, to the branching of ministerial work into formal pastoral counseling, to the acceptance of alcoholism as an illness and the swift rise of chemical dependency as a treatable problem, to the development and description of some 250 or so separate kinds of therapy for every emotional or psychological symptom from which man has ever suffered, no social movement, in my view, has undergone more change.

And since change requires adaptation from a creature that generally enjoys the status quo, anyone who has been living and working with our care systems for a while probably can't get his head to stop spinning. Nor is he likely to.

Who is in the middle of all this swirling change? You, the manager.

Since good change doesn't happen without help, anyone who becomes a manager becomes an agent of change. To be intellectually prepared and positively disposed to the idea that change is coming, is inevitable, and (here's the important part) needs *your* help is, in my view, the only possible way a manager can survive in a world where someone is inventing a new wheel two or three times a week. A manager can either learn how to help change along, rise to the task of creating her own changes, participate in the products and policies that change requires, or, frankly, she should stay out of the kitchen.

The most miserable managers I know are people who automatically resist every suggestion that a change may be necessary. Their first response to some new requirement or intake form or procedure, is, "It can't be done!" Or, "This is an impossibility!"

Why?

"Because no one ever did it that way before?"

This attitude may be okay if you are hand building fine watches in Switzerland and have been doing so since the fifteenth century, but for a modern-day manager to dig in her heels over a tradition that dates all the way back to—let's be generous and say last year—is hardly the sort of risk taking, exploratory, let's-see-if-we-can-do-it-this-way sort of person your boss needs to take on the job of designing the new wheel we need by next Friday.

This does not mean that a manager should not question the latest request for change or raise concerns about its implications, but it does mean that in spite of our desires for things to remain constant and stable long enough to get a day's work done, people-helping institutions are still evolving at a high rate of speed and, unless I miss my guess, they won't settle down into any sort of comfortable routines until midway into the next century—at which time people will probably look back on our era with the same mixture of humor and horror with which we look back on the medicine and magic of the 1880s.

Because change is so much a part of a manager's job, I'm devoting the next chapter to how you might do it better.

There are many more responsibilities that come with the unwritten job of the people-helper manager and I hope, throughout the rest of this book, to touch on them as they come up. But because this chapter is getting too long for good taste, I'll quit here.

3

Helping Change Happen

I have already alluded to the need for a manager to become an agent of change. Simply put, you either adopt an attitude that change *can* be good or, as I see it, you are probably in the wrong job. Unless you learn to help change happen, you may unwittingly add to the sometimes high cost change extracts from your agency.

For example, consider the following typical management problem.

Due to a change in funding patterns (a grant ends, higher authorities change the priorities for the agency, etc.) a team of ten people helpers are asked to make the following adjustments:

- Work slightly different hours (come in an hour later, leave an hour later).
- Work for a new manager who is known, by reputation, to be a good, fair, and competent manager.
- Move into a different set of offices. These offices are, in many ways, better than the ones they left.

After a meeting between the team and the new manager during which duties, types of clients, and skills required are thoroughly discussed, everyone seems ready to take on the new challenge. Training and orientation for the slightly different work they will be doing is quite thorough. There are no changes in salary or benefits; in fact, one of the line staff will be promoted to a supervisory position as a result of the change.

Within the first month, one of the team members resigns.

Question: Within *one year* from the date the change was required and implemented, how many of the ten staff members remain?

While you're picking a number, I will pass on some disheartening news for managers in our field. Turnover is high. From the Bureau of National Affairs data (1987 figures), health care turnover runs 18 percent; compared to 14.4 percent in non-manufacturing, 15.6 percent in nonbusiness, and 13.2 percent in all companies. Briefly put, health-care workers come and go at a significantly higher rate than other kinds of workers.

While I have no good figures for the mental health industry, I'm told by personnel experts in this field that mental-health workers turnover even more rapidly than their colleagues in general health care. Length of stay (how long the average new hire stays on the job), is as low as two or three years. In some cases staff stay with an agency less time than the clients the agency serves.

To the degree change is responsible for this high turnover, I want to explore the subject of change and how you might be able to help change happen in ways that do not result in an excess of stress, anxiety, job dissatisfaction, and unnecessary resignations from your agency.

For the record, I am not certain that change is the culprit in the turnover problem in human service work. It could be many things; so-called burnout, better opportunities in other fields, competition for qualified employees between the public and private sectors, lack of good management practices by people-helper managers, or any number of other factors or combination of factors.

I am fairly certain that any time you ask staff to do something different you are tampering with their habits—most of which have become as comfortable as an old pair of loafers. And though people don't like others to fool around with their comfort zones (and especially people whose training and education has encouraged a fierce sense of autonomy and independence), change demands it. Getting change accomplished is the way managers earn their salaries.

Now back to my question. How many of the ten staffers will be left at the end of a year following the change requirements I listed?

Training groups of managers given this hypothetical situation from which to make a prediction have responded as follows:

Recently promoted managers: seven or eight staff will still be on the payroll at year's end.

Old hands: only two or three will be left.

A few real old hands: zero.

Having watched this process several times, I would have to vote with the old hands. Despite our best-laid plans and highest hopes that a significant staff change will not decimate the existing work force, it seems to anyway. But I'm not convinced that it has to.

Because the price of change is so high to clients, remaining staff, the agency, and its mission, I will try to describe for you what I hope will be some useful ways to help change along.

First, let's examine how we think about workers. Before you can expect workers to go along with change, it might be useful to conduct a quick self-analysis of your own attitudes toward workers, you know, the "little" people.

One Set of Assumptions
- people hate work (any kind of work)
- people are basically lazy
- threats are necessary to get people to work
- workers need to be told what to do
- though they say they do, most workers don't want responsibility

If you agree with some or any of the above beliefs about workers, then your job as a change agent should be fairly simple. You just step up to the task, give direct orders, and see to it that everyone does what he's told. If a few people leave well, hell, you didn't create the world or its survival requirements.

This sort of thinking is part of the top-down management philosophy of the screaming capitalist and, so long as you have a large pool of unemployed workers with the skills you need to do the jobs you need done, you can, in fact, afford to think of and treat people in this fashion. Capitalism thrives on a high unemployment rate—at least in the short term. If a few bodies get strewn along the way it is, after all, just business. I need not go into the consequences of this sort of attitude in a tight labor market.

As an aside, I am occasionally amazed at how some people recently arrived in management with a brand-new title and bursting with authority suddenly revert to this kind of power-broker-boss-of-industry thinking about the people who now work *for* them. Fortunately, such people don't last long in our institutions, or if they do they have a tough time keeping people.

Personally, I make it a point never to promote people who drool slightly when they get a whiff of power. Leave such a person "in charge" for a day or two and, unless you're sound asleep, your staff will remind you of something Plato once said a long time ago: "Access to power must be confined to men who are not in love with it."

Another Set of Assumptions about People
- people like to work
- people like to solve problems
- people enjoy innovation
- people are not lazy—rather, the human creature is a curious one, driven by a multitude of complicated psychological needs, one of the most important of which is to do productive, meaningful work
- people can make important decisions and want to take responsibility for their work

If this is the way you think about your staff, you're going to find helping change happen almost fun. You might be disappointed by a couple of people, but that is okay—the rest of the staff should rise to your positive expectations of them. (If you don't think this way about workers and never can, then maybe you had best skip to the chapter "An Inward Look" and analyze your own work and leadership style—it might prove instructive.)

In keeping with my ten-point plan (that anything worth talking about should require no more than ten points), I'm going to list the steps I think are necessary to help change happen with a minimum of, as the Germans say, Sturm und Drang.

1. Learn why a change is needed.

After you've accepted the idea that you are an active change agent, get yourself educated. To help change along, you need to know all you possibly can about the whys and wherefores of the change that is being made. Who is requesting it? Why do they want the change now? What are the forces driving the change? Economic? Political? Regulatory? A shift in priorities? You need, as the verb *background* emerges into our language, the best possible backgrounding you can get.

Why? Because your staff will ask you why, as in, "But why do we have to do it this way?"

If you don't know why you are asking them to do something different, you've immediately set yourself up as some sort of automaton who takes directives blindly and who clearly hasn't enough inside information to explain the reasons why the change is needed. If you say to them, "I'm not sure why, just do it" you will lose round one, and maybe the whole contest.

Since clinicians and counselors work with human motivation for a living and are frequently asked the why question by both their clients and supervisors on a daily basis, it seems only natural (to me anyway) that they would have a high need to know why something is changing. If you don't give them the best explanation you can, they tend to get paranoid and start dreaming up their own reasons for why some change is being required of them.

And since the only thing harder than supervising a group of paranoids is working for one, never underestimate the staff's need for the "inside scoop." Getting the inside scoop can put their fears to rest and, besides, it's something they expect and deserve from you.

People love to be a part of the place they work. They like to know the details (preferably sordid, I've found) of what's *happening*, and anything you can do to include them in will help your cause when you've got to ask them to make a change.

Withholding information may give you a sense of power, but you will pay a dear price for the practice. Because once your staff discovers you've been less than candid about something that did not require all that much candor, their trust in you will diminish and you may find yourself trying to supervise a bunch of paranoids.

Finally, your job as a manager is to either speak the company's line, or help the company establish a line you can speak. Waffle, stumble, take a position ten degrees off what needs to be communicated, and change will be that much more difficult.

2. Get everyone on board.

Try to include *all* the players who will be affected by some change in the process of change itself. This does not mean you need to conduct a public vote about whether the required change is good or bad or makes sense for everyone, it just means that the more people included in the explanation and education phases of the required change, the better luck you will have in building a positive consensus and the less likely some will see themselves as being the victim of change.

Since people don't resist change nearly so much as being changed ("Someone is doing it to me again!"), it is worth the investment of time to try to get everyone on board well ahead of the date the change is due.

The bigger the change required, the more time should be taken to tease out staff concerns, fears, or other sources of resistance. Over the years, our agency has approved so-called staff planning days to help with the implementation of major changes. Although work sessions, these meetings take place away from the agency in someone's lakeside home or at a resort or some other place where the atmosphere is casual and there are no interruptions. When the work is done and a consensus has been built, everyone can let down and have some food and fun.

Since some people helpers like to feel special, it may be necessary to work one-on-one with a key person who has a high need to be in on the ground floor. When I know a big change is coming, and if I have one of these people on my staff. I might drop into their office, swear them to secrecy, and then let them in on what's about to happen.

3. Give the details of implementation away.

Exactly *how* a change will take place is at least as critical to making a successful change as building a consensus that the change is needed. In a word, to buy into the change and feel some ownership in whatever new is being required, you need the staff to become a part of the process of just *how* a new thing will be done.

For example, if a new program is leaving the drawing board and headed for implementation it will need, most likely, a set of referral procedures, new forms, and a schedule of how services and events will be delivered. If you've made your request for change clear (e.g., we need to start a new group therapy program for depressed teenagers that will serve a hundred kids a year), you should be able to leave the *how* of it up to the staff. Requiring only final approval, let them design the intake forms, the referral forms, write the procedures, and set the schedules.

This delegation of the work of change is so important I've devoted an entire chapter to the concept and how, I hope, to do it well. My point here, however, is to stress that when you give power and responsibility away, you get back commitment. And when you are working your way through some change or other, you will need all the commitment you can get.

4. Dates and timetables.

If you don't set dates certain for the implementation of a change, don't be disappointed when nothing happens. For reasons best known to only the gods, people-helper staff never seem to quite realize how urgent some change is and will, without time frames, drift along with a certain enviable nonchalance that, usually, drives us managers mad.

But this is our own fault. It is our job to set expectations, specific dates, and to be clear about just what it is we want and when we want it. If the date of implementing some new change doesn't matter all that much, let staff decide when the change over to the new regime is to take place (ownership, again). But if the timing does matter, then explain why it matters and don't mince words about when you expect to see the change implemented.

5. Keep everyone posted.

If, as they say in the business manager's world, "feedback is the breakfast of champions" it is no less true when managing people helpers. Routine reports on how a new change is going are very important to the process of good change. You may think staff are bored by this kind of management reporting in their meetings, but you'd be wrong. Again, people like to be on the inside. They like to be a part of a tight, well-functioning team. They like, more than anything else, to be stroked for helping to get a difficult job done.

Maybe more important, the sharing of change information and keeping people posted lets everyone know that you are concerned about how the change may be affecting them and, where possible, you may be able to make adjustments in the process or fine-tune procedures or run interference for them with another program. The few minutes it takes to file a report in a staff meeting also makes it possible for people to bring up concerns or worries.

Lastly, by handling today's change well with a reliable feedback loop, implementing tomorrow's change will be that much easier. (And there will be a change tomorrow . . . , you can take it to the bank.)

6. Stay mindful of training needs.

Occasionally a change will require staff to develop or learn new skills. It is only fair that if new skills are required by staff some thought be given as to just how these will be acquired. Formal classes, bringing in an outside consultant or trainer, or teaching the skills yourself—all of these are possibilities.

In my experience, some staff are unable to learn the skills they need to do a new job. The job may be too big for them or require a quality of cognitive thinking they do not possess. Sometimes the new job obliges them to work with a client group with whom they have little empathy or, worse, for whom they have a frank antipathy. Such circumstances are unfortunate and unless the person can be transferred to a more compatible program or position, you will probably lose him.

Since knowledge overcomes fear of the unknown (and people resist change precisely because its consequences are unknown), no time and money spent on helping staff overcome their feelings of the unknown in a new job will be wasted. Once competence is achieved by training and experience, things should settle back down to more comfortable routines.

7. Be a model of risk taking.

To overcome the inertia of habit that change requires, it is important that you, as manager, be seen by staff as the sort of person who is willing to take a chance. As managers I feel we have a right to ask people to take risks and try new things; we, therefore, can't afford to be sticks in the mud ourselves.

Here's my favorite gag on this "try it, you might like it" idea.

Two managers stop by a deli for lunch. One of the managers sees that tongue sandwiches are on special.

"I've never tried a tongue sandwich," he says. "It might be good. Anything's worth trying once." And he orders the tongue sandwich.

The other manager says, "A tongue sandwich!!? Yuukkk! Are you crazy? How can you possibly eat something that comes out of the mouth of an animal!!?" Then he orders the egg salad.

For my part, give me a manager willing to try the tongue sandwich.

8. Change should reduce burdens, not increase them.

However you must do it, it is important that early on you and your counterparts on the management team make every effort to see to it that any necessary change, in fact, results in some benefit—either to staff or to clients. If a change means more paperwork, it had also better mean more benefits for clients. If a switch over to a computer-based data system will mean less work for staff in the long run, then be convinced (and convincing) while you are selling them on the idea.

One of the major reasons people resist change (other than pure, unadulterated human stubbornness) is that they feel they will be asked to do more work, never less. To overcome this built-in, shockproof, stainless-steel belief, you must overwhelm them with stories about how easy life will be once, say, they have learned to dictate their reports.

Sometimes, though, a bureaucrat in some outside regulatory

agency will dream up some cockeyed form they need filled out and, unencumbered by the realities of clinical work, this form will be a world-class example of time-wasting stupidity. Worse, since agency compliance may be tied to funding (read, life-blood), filling the form out may be unavoidable. After you've fought the good fight and lost, and there is nothing left to do but to do it, then tell the troops the way it is and tell them, too, that you expect them to do it right, on time, and with the same level of dedication they do everything else. Reality, as we are often prone to say to our clients, isn't always pleasant, but it is always real.

9. What's final is never really final.

The phrase, "We're going to try this for a while and see how it works" will do more to ease people's mind about change than anything else. This is why, no doubt, pilot projects, thirty-day trials and such are so popular. Setting expectations that the change is fluid, may be altered in significant ways, and (best of all), the final procedures or product will need your (the staff's) personal input, should make the whole process more palatable.

Of course no final decision is ever truly final, even when we'd like one to be. The form and shape of our organizations are in a constant state of growth and change, expansion and contraction and redirection, and, with all of this amoebiclike activity, the paperwork, forms, procedures, documents, and people must change as well. The only way I know to avoid the change going on in the health care industry is to get out and into something like harness making.

10. Take care of the last man.

Anytime a big change is required, and if you go through the steps I have suggested, you may, despite your best efforts, encounter what I like to call the last man—as in, "We're willing to fight and die to the last man. And here I am!"

This "Over my dead body!" quality of resistance can best be handled in a one-on-one session. In a staff meeting where a change is being discussed, such people will often lean back, fold their arms, set their jaws, and attempt to lead the others in a quiet revolt against the change you are asking for. It seems to be a matter of principal with them, as if challenging authority at every juncture of change was a moral obligation. Jeremiahs in their predictions of doom (there is always power in prophesying catastrophe), they take it upon themselves to lead the noble opposition.

This is fine and, often, some of their predictions may come true. However (and this is a big *however*) such people never seem to have an alternative suggestion as to how to solve whatever problem the change is trying to solve. Ask them, "Well, how do you suggest we do it better?" and you will get nothing. They may even say, "I don't get paid enough to solve these kinds of problems." Or, "That's what they pay you for."

If the change is being required by external forces (an outside funding source for example), such people will imply that you, as the manager, have not done a good job of defending the staff. "You're not going to let 'them' get away with this, are you?" seems to be the real unspoken question. And the message is, "You haven't any real power, you're just a wimp and beneath contempt."

Knowing that the optimists will take care of themselves and the skeptics will come around eventually, this oppositional last-man attitude presents a considerable problem. If I cannot win him over with facts, convincing logical arguments, or that the change is necessary for the good of the client or the agency, or by any other reasonable effort, then, as I see it, I have only one choice.

That choice (since I cannot march him out to a convenient wall and have him shot), is to take him to task about his oppositional attitude, his apparent unwillingness to go along with change requests, his inability to be a team player, and, ultimately, his fitness to do his job. This is, I know, drastic action. But considering the manager's obligations to his staff, his boss, his agency, and his community of clients, the resistance and morale problems created by the last man are simply not tolerable.

When one of my sons was going through that phase of early teenage development where this attitude typically rears its head, I once said to him, "Your automatic refusal to cut the lawn after my first request is a good example of what we psychologists call oppositional behavior."

To which he replied, dryly, "There is no such thing as oppositional behavior."

I will submit to you that since a manager doesn't have time to help an automatically resistant staff member out of his teenage years and past this particular developmental phase, some other kind of action may be required. (See chapter on firing.)

There are doubtless many more aspects to facilitating change, but together with whatever training you may have had as a therapist or counselor or clinician, you should, by dint of this training, have the necessary skills to help change along even better than the average business person. As a trained listener, accurate empathizer, and all-round nice person, you already have the basics.

My guess, though, is that what feels uncomfortably heavy during the process of change is the mantle of authority. Because, being the boss, and if you have to, you simply must oblige people to do what they're told. Or else.

Since this ugly necessity to give direct orders is a heresy to most trained people helpers, the actual wielding of raw power is the hardest thing you may ever have to do. But sometimes it is exactly what the mission requires. And so long as you have your eye on the ball and the client's welfare foremost in your mind, you will, I think, find the courage to act.

4

Planning and Goal Setting

Y our first reaction to reading the title of this chapter was probably a yawn and a "So what?" That was certainly my reaction to the idea of writing it. But because the business of planning and goal setting are so important to the operation of your agency or hospital or institution, I'm going to run through the basics and, if I can, make the subject as interesting as possible.

A Dream with Wheels

Have you wondered what might have happened to the civil rights movement if, during his most famous speech, Martin Luther King, Jr., had declared, "I have a plan!" instead of "I have a dream!"

Two things come immediately to mind: the general level of paranoia among white people would have jumped ten points, and J. Edgar Hoover would have doubled the number of G-men assigned to the Luther case.

But a dream? Oh, sure, anyone can dream. A dream is something you can always wake up from. A dream, all by itself, won't get you from point A to point B, let alone to the end of the alphabet.

A plan, though, is something else again. A plan (from the epigrammatic pen) is a dream with wheels.

Without a means of getting from idea to action, the best dreams and visions of the future are just so much fluff. When our client dreams without a plan, we call it a fantasy. When our client dreams big dreams without a plan, we call it a delusion. I don't know what you call it when you dream dreams, but when I dream I call it conceptualizing a deliberate future. (They don't give you a PhD to go around using little words, now do they?)

As a manager of the people who will help accomplish the mission of your agency you are, at least in part, responsible for putting wheels under the dream. You must somehow envision a deliberate future, plan how to arrive there, and then take the necessary action. While you may not be involved in the overall direction the agency takes, you are surely involved in putting and keeping some of the small wheels under the dream.

Nothing That Different

The idea of planning should not be new to clinicians and counselors. We are used to making plans. We made plans to get where we are professionally. Every day we work with clients we help them make plans to get where they want to go. As long as your frontal lobes are intact and functional, you should be able to plan.

I once read (but don't remember where) that many of the most successful leaders of industry and business are great planners. Presented with a decision, they begin to cogitate on the consequences of the various courses of action available to them should they decide in favor of A versus B. Similarly, they then imagine the consequences of pursuing B. In their mind's eye, they can foresee (better than most) where each choice will eventually lead them over the coming weeks or months or years.

At the same time they are processing these possible outcomes, they are assessing their resources, strengths, the environments through which the consequences of the decisions must travel, and the people in the organization who must push the new mission forward. Once all the data have been considered, the outcomes anticipated and the resources lined up, the final act is to set the whole plan into motion.

From ship's captains, to the wagon masters of the American West, to General Eisenhower's grand plan to invade Europe on the beaches of Normandy, the process is essentially the same. It occurs in four steps:

- a statement of the mission (why are we going?)
- the setting the goals (where are we going?)
- the spelling out of specific objectives (what are the things we must achieve along the way to get where we want to go?)
- specifying the actions and activities (what must we *do* to get there?)

Nothing should be new or different or strange about planning. Unless you're the sort of person who arrives at the supermarket hungry and just starts down isle A, you don't need to be convinced of the desirability of a shopping list. All of us need short-term plans just to get through the day.

However, planning for the long term seems to be in short supply, not just among us managers, but also throughout the bureaucratic systems in which we work. So-called long-range, strategic planning is all too rare in the social service field and, unless I miss my guess, you have, more than once, suffered from short-range, nonstrategic planning or, as it is more commonly called by funding sources, "one-time-only money." Except for those moneys spent to answer reasonably asked research questions, one-time-only money is the funding equivalent of Alka-Seltzer—you get a little relief but no real cure.

Here's something to think about: if you don't plan your own deliberate future, someone will plan it for you. This may sound a little paranoid, but in the human service and health care industry, a little paranoia in a manager is a healthy thing—that is, if you like surviving. Any manager or CEO who has opened the office mail one morning to find a brand-new "Plan for the Future" dreamed up by some regulatory, funding, or governmental body knows what I'm talking about.

This is not to say that high-level planners don't know how to do their jobs; rather, it has been my experience that the work of competent planners is often ignored by the people with the most power and the best political connections. These latter folks are more than willing to describe the shape of the future without, apparently, the encumbrance of detailed projections as to the long-range effects of their decisions. In the kindest terms possible, many of the grand plans I've seen come down the pipe appear to have sponsored by some rare form of brain fever.

Remembering the old saw that nothing is impossible for those who don't have to do it, inventing and driving your own plans can be the equivalent of taking charge of your professional life.

Enough digressions. . . .

In my own view, step one (the mission statement) can be very short. The goals and objectives are best stated simply as well. The action plan (what you will actually do to get there) can be long or short, but short is always better.

The whole plan needn't be elaborate, complicated, or detailed. In fact, the more work you intend to delegate (so that others can have a part in putting wheels under the dream) the shorter the plan can be. You should be able to type up a reasonably good plan of action to justify the expenditure of several thousands dollars of human resources on no more than a few sheets of paper, usually less.

Multimillion-dollar state or federal grants are one thing, but a few thousand dollars to start a program to help seventy-five families a year with a staff of three, an office, and a typewriter is nothing to work up a sweat about.

In the early days of my work in the mental health movement I can remember a time when, as some new money became available, I could dictate a proposal (plan) over the phone to the funding source—complete with mission statement, goals, objectives, people resources needed, and budget justifications—all in a matter of a few minutes. Unfortunately, given all the rules, regulations, accountants, lawyers, and paperwork requirements that have accompanied the maturation of the system, it takes a little longer now. But the process is still the same.

Setting Goals and Objectives

Here are a few simple rules for setting goals and objectives. If there is, by the way, an important difference between a goal and an objective, it has always escaped me. Despite considerable training in management-by-objectives procedures, I remain confused about the distinction. For me, goals are bigger, objectives are littler. I figure my boss sets goals, I set objectives.

Back to the rules.

1. Keep goals measurable.

As much as I may hate counting beans, there is still only one way to ever know how many beans you have. Therefore, if you are going to increase the number of clients seen in counseling by adding one new staff member, how many more clients are you going to see?

After setting any program goal, ask yourself: How are we going to measure this? If your answer is obvious and inexpensive to get, you've met the first criterion of a good goal.

2. Keep goals simple.

Since you are going to end up counting something to see if you've achieved your objective, keep the keeping track as simple as you can. In my experience, funding sources, boards, and auditors, prefer the plans with the fewest working parts.

For example, if you are planning to improve the quality and quantity of services to alcohol-abusing teenagers, just say how many kids you will see, how many hours of service you will deliver, how long you will be able to see the kids, and who, in terms of staff, will do the work. If you can keep track of how many kids improved as a result of your efforts, so much the better. But don't fall into the trap of trying to answer the why question.

The why question, often posed by people who do not understand the nature and difficulty of human subjects research, is the one question you should never offer to answer in your plan—unless, of course, you are a researcher. "Why does your proposed therapy program work better than any one else's? Why do the kids you see run away from home in the first place? Why are so many women in your clinic depressed?"

A word of advice: Leave the why questions to the research people in the universities. Or, as a wise old manager once said, "Promise them as little as possible and JUST GET THE MONEY!"

Easily measured simple goals are the best way to get money for services and to keep that money coming. The same is true for any planning you must do.

The planner who states his goal is to stop kids drinking, reduce adolescent crime rates, put an end to one-car accidents, stop teen pregnancy, favorably impact the educational system, and cause mothers and fathers to rejoice throughout the catchment area, has (unless they're giving him ten zillion dollars) set himself up for failure. And everyone, including the funding source, will be disappointed.

3. Give goals timetables.

Objectives without dates and times by which they should be reached are just so much pie in the sky. If you set a time for a thing to be done, it will get done or you will know the reason why—provided, of course, you've a fail-safe process in place to follow up what you think you put into motion. If a clear deadline guarantees reaching a goal, a fuzzy one guarantees missing it.

   4. Give goals priorities.

Every plan requires setting priorities. You have several objectives to achieve, people to achieve them by certain times, and the means to reach the goal. What do you do first?

Again, simply jotting down the steps to be taken will set the priority list for you. Let's say you are responsible to plan a new program for rape victims. You have already determined that a need exists and your mission statement reads as follows: To locate, assist, and provide therapeutic and supportive services to rape victims of any age or sex.

You've got a green light to develop the program. Your priority work list could look like this:

- Get the money.
- Make sure of the money.
- Make absolutely sure of the money.
- Develop a referral network (police department, hospitals, etc.).
- Set a program start date.
- On or before September 1, get media coverage for new program and begin recruiting volunteers.
- On or before September 15, advertise for staff.
- On or before October 15, have staff hired.
- Somewhere around October 16, start looking for offices for new staff.

(A really good planner would make sure she had offices for new staff before she hired them, but that would take an awful lot of the fun out the joys of planning, wouldn't it?)

- By no later than October 31, have staff oriented, trained and ready to go.
- November 1: see first clients.

(I might note here that a really good planner starts scheduling clients for a new staffer *before* the new staffer actually moves into her office. That way the day she comes to work she can start seeing clients right off. I once pulled this with a new psychiatrist who, two hours after he had settled into his office, got to meet his first patient. "You don't give a guy much rest around here, do you?" he asked. "No," I said, "but thanks for the compliment.")

- Start counting beans (events, hours of service, numbers of clients, modalities used, etc., etc.). This is the evaluation phase and should begin on the same day the new program begins.

The best way to set the priority list of Things to Do is rough one out, go over it with staff or supervisor, get input, and refine as you go.

5. Keep goals achievable.

Goals you simply can't reach kill motivation. While you want your people to stretch a bit to reach the objective you've set, you don't want them to say, "Hells bells, the boss is delusional again!"

Setting goals for the delivery of human services is often a best-guess thing. Experienced hands know this and so, even if you pick numbers and outcomes you think you can achieve and you miss them by a wide margin, it shouldn't be the end of the world—especially if you've asked for a little leeway in your projections. I've set dozens of goals for staff projects and programs that were so far off the mark you'd think I did my planning in a opium den, and not once did someone order that I be taken out and summarily shot.

Actions and Activities

When I began this book I promised myself not to delve (deeply anyway) into that dark motivational box called human behavior, or to try to answer the question "Why do people work anyway?"

But somehow we must get, lead, or help staff to actually do that which has been prescribed by way of our goals and objectives. And while there are many ways to do this (and I've touched on a few throughout this text) I would only add here that when it comes to pinpointing what it is we need to count, monitor, and reward, no one does this better than the behavioral psychologists. In this regard, I've listed a couple of behavioral management texts in the resource appendix and can recommend both.

A Few Final Comments

There isn't really all that much difference between setting goals for clients and setting goals for the work of the agency. With clients the process is evaluation, diagnosis, intervention, and reassessment. With agency work it is needs assessment, planning, monitoring, and reassessment. The critical question seems to be: Where do you want to go, how will you get there, and how will you know when you've arrived?

Answer these questions and your planning is done.

I believe quite strongly that to be a successful manager you must have dreams with wheels and a road map to follow. Why you want to go where you want to go is up to you and your agency, but as a delightful and temporarily confused client once told me, "When I'm lost, I don't where I'm going." If any of us hopes to avoid getting lost we must become proactive in planning our own deliberate futures.

Finally, it is not enough just to see to it that your staff get their work done, that they get paid on time, and that you are there to handle questions and special problems. This may be a form of leadership, but all the planning such a reactive leader needs is the postscript "Keep your heads down and your ammo dry." Such status quo managing is hardly inspiring and is only fitting for agency's already fossilized by inaction.

To be a reactive manager in a field as changeable, faddish, unstable, and fraught with regulatory peril as our own is to forfeit our future to the guy willing to do our thinking for us. And these guys are out there. Lots of them. Many of them are not trained people helpers and wouldn't know a client if they fell over one. But that doesn't mean they don't *know best* what our clients need, how the work should be done, when it should be done, by whom, and for how much. And if we think the quality of their thinking greatly exceeds the quality of our own thinking, then we are probably being overpaid.

To realize the mission and dream of our agencies, we must see to it that the work is done efficiently, effectively, on schedule, and at a consistently high level of quality. We must be able to defend our services, their true costs, the relevance of what we do, and the importance of the work we do as regards our own communities. If what we do is good for humanity, that is okay too. But the era of getting paid for just being "a nice human being who wants to do good things in the world" ended about twenty years ago and there is no going back. Accountability is in, good intentions are insufficient. To accomplish the mission and keep things going, we must be able to plan the work and carry it out in a timely, cost-effective manner.

To get the work done well, you will need the commitment of your staff. To get the kind of commitment you need, the staff needs a vision as clear as yours and a plan to work by. This planning is your job.

More, a dream with big rolling wheels is empowering. When the staff realize they are part of an important, worthwhile and, yes, even noble enterprise, the work of an agency flows smoothly, steadily, and always out of an atmosphere that seems charged with that certain special something.

Energy? Enthusiasm? Esprit de corps? Whatever it is, you can feel it and, to the degree you can get it going and keep it going where you work, you may find yourself getting up in the morning with that can't-wait-to-get-to-work feeling.

5

Management Tools

Enough of theory. The best-laid plans, goals, objectives, and all the inspiration in the world won't get the house built until someone comes up with the hammer and nails. This chapter is about hammers and nails.

Because at least some readers may be working in relatively small shops, I'm going to break things down here into two broad areas: low-budget tools and high-budget tools. The first set of tools every manager can afford to own, the second set require a pretty fancy computer and the softwear to run it.

Low-Budget Management Tools

The most expensive management tool at your agency's disposal it already owns—you. You are the high-priced hammer and most of the nails. All you need to do is to learn how to use yourself.

Without getting off into the nether world of more management theory, a manager can only be effective if she has information. Accurate information. And lots of it. Since it has been pointed out that information is power, I don't see how you can ever have too much information. Until you have the facts, figures, and personal knowledge to truly understand some problem or other, I fail to see how you, as a manager, can make decent decisions.

This is not to say that we ever have all the information we need to make perfect decisions. No one ever does. What matters, though, is that a manager be able to act on the best information available—however limited and incomplete it may be. The trick is to get that information.

There are many ways to gather information and, because I feel strongly that the best managers operate from positions of high knowledge, all of the ideas that follow stem from this central premise: good information = good intelligence = good decisions.

Listening

For a couple of years when I was a young man I was a trained eavesdropper. I listened for a living. The people I listened to probably knew I was there, but they couldn't do anything about it. Trained by the US Army Security Agency, I was assigned the inglorious duty of listening in on the radio transmissions of our enemies at that time in history, cold war enemies who are now practically our pals. I typed down what I heard and handed the data over to the really bright guys in our outfit (mostly Harvard chaps) who then sorted things out and made sense of the "priority traffic."

A good manager listens. To everything and everybody. In the so-called walk-around model of management, the manager is out on the floor with his people, listening, asking questions, helping out, troubleshooting on the spot. This is on-line, in-the-field management and, while it might work well in some settings, it is not so easily accomplished in many human service settings, although nurses get it done better than most.

My main point here is not that you, as manager, are out there working the floor, guiding and directing the action, but rather that you are out there where you can *hear* things. You can't hear things from behind a closed office door.

Any Information Is Good Information

In my job as a low-grade spy, I was what was called a general search operator. On each duty shift a general search operator was assigned a specific band of radio frequencies. His job was to scan, again and again, this band of frequencies, listen to any and all transmissions, and stay with them until they were identified as nonpriority traffic, after which the search began again. (Hot items in those days were Russian submarines, Russian space flights, Chinese missile launches, and sundry spy-network radio transmissions.)

In a way, you need to become a general search operator. If you go directly to your office each morning and only venture out to attend meetings you will, more or less automatically, shut yourself off from important sources of priority traffic. If you leave your door open, a certain amount of information will flow through, but only from those souls brave enough to come into the boss's office.

If, however, you walk around a bit, stop and chat with folks, share a story with the mantainence man, and pop into other people's office for a cup of coffee, you will (given that you understand this is *work* and not just shooting the breeze) gather a great deal of important information. You will be operating a kind of general search for bits of intelligence.

Every agency, every social organization has what are called key informants. Key informants are people who make it a point to be in the know. They know what's cooking. Sometimes gossips, more often they thrive on and help sustain a rich communication network whose existence is supported by a steady flow of reliable information about the life of the organization. These folks are usually centrally positioned in this river of intelligence and, more than anyone else, know who, what, where, when, and sometimes even the why of what's going down. You need to know and listen to this person.

The key informant for operations large and small is usually the receptionist/secretary or the PBX operator or whoever it is who keeps track of the whereabouts of the staff. In a hospital it may be the ward clerk. In small agencies it is almost always the receptionist/secretary. In larger organizations it may be the administrative assistant, or the personnel chief. It doesn't matter where this person works, it only matters that you, as a manager, listen to the intelligence your fellow general search operator collects.

The intelligence may be rumor, wrong or wicked. Quality doesn't matter. You can sort out the purpose, meaning, and merit of the data later. But you must know things like the following:

- That clients are complaining about having to wait too long for their appointments.
- That if the air conditioner quits one more time in Dr. Brown's office he's going to start looking for a different job. (Dr. Brown will hint his dissatisfaction to the PBX operator long before he complains to his director about something as mundane as a malfunctioning air conditioner.)
- That Ms. Priss (the new therapist) treats the medical records staff like a bunch of idiots and they are "losing" her charts and causing her even more distemper.
- That one of your staff has been seen closing down a certain nightclub six nights a week, which may, by the way, account for why he's been coming in late on Monday mornings for the last few months and asking the reception staff to cover for him.
- That Dr. Smith (who is married) is sleeping with Mrs. Barlow (who is also married) and that while the affair is widely known about by staff and patients (who can spot a lovesick gaze across a crowded room as well as the next person) neither Mrs. Smith nor Mr. Barlow has a clue; the word going around is that "when the lid blows off this one it's going to rain lawsuits for a week."

I am not suggesting that you become an intentional part of your agency's rumor mill. You don't have to pass on a single thing you hear. But I am suggesting that you need to hear what's happening—if only to prepare yourself for eventualities, to not be "shocked" when the lid blows off the Smith-Barlow affair, and to be in a position to take preemptive action on a host of things that managers often hear about only after it is too late.

There is, in my view, what I will call the period of perfect timing. This is the time window during which an action by a manager will have its greatest chance of success. During this period, the best possible outcome can be achieved with the least-possible hassle. But you have to act. And you can only act *if* you have the information.

You may not be able to do much about the Smith-Barlow

affair, but you can certainly do something about the client complaints of waiting too long, the Ms. Priss who is aggravating the medical records staff, the air conditioner, and the staff member whose drinking is out of control. The better your information network and the broader your general search, the more little problems you'll hear about and be able to head off before they become big problems.

Call such an information network by any name you like, the only rule for keeping it going is never to betray your sources. When people ask me how I hear about problems I've come to them to help them solve, I just say, "Oh, you know, I've got a pretty good grapevine. It's part of my job."

The Weekly Staff Meeting

Another low-budget management tool already in place is the regularly scheduled weekly staff meeting. As opposed to the clinical supervision meeting, the weekly staff meeting should be an administrative meeting that serves the broad goals of the agency. This meeting should help people keep answering the question, "How are we doing, anyway?"

This meeting is a time specifically set aside to listen, ask questions, monitor, evaluate, and keep track of what's going on with clients, staff, the program, its goals and objectives, and the problems everyone has. The topics can be as narrow as a billing procedure or as wide-ranging as how some new program will fit into the broader community. Team building, mutual support, the latest joke, and trading recipes for barbecue—all of these things are the legitimate ingredients of the weekly staff meeting.

I cannot overstress this point: Never treat this meeting casually, cancel it without very good cause, or in any way diminish its importance.

Why? Because this is the meeting that helps everyone keep his eye on the ball, helps everyone feel a part of something bigger than himself, and the meeting in which, despite how you may personally feel about the time it takes, meets a lot of essential human needs. The needs for affiliation, for inside information, to be a player in some grand scheme, for friendship, for contact with others like oneself, to have an hour or two out of the week when client demands are safely shelved while we take care of our own. I repeat, never treat this meeting lightly.

The Sick-Leave Report

Years ago I encountered the following problem. Consider it a manager's mystery.

Two afternoons a month a certain staff person went home sick. Headache. Flu. The sniffles. Something. This person reported to one of my supervisors, but he was unaware there was a problem and never brought it to my attention. And I would not have known there was a problem either, except that the therapist missing so much work turned up on the sick-leave report. This was my first clue.

A low-budget sick-leave report includes the following bits of information:

- who used sick leave in the last month or ninety-day interval
- how many times (hours) of sick leave were used during the report interval
- how many total days (hours) has the person used year-to-date
- total days (hours) used year ending . . . (prior year) for each person on the report

This is pretty unsophisticated data. Payroll should be able to give it to you, if it is not already provided on a routine basis. If you don't now have access to this prime source of intelligence about your staff, I'd strongly recommend you start getting it.

You will notice I used the term *sick leave used* with no implication that the person was actually sick. Being sick is fine and most everyone gets to feeling puny once in a while, but calling in "sick" is very different from having a high fever and being unable to hold down your breakfast.

Absenteeism is a broader term and better fits all the reasons people miss work and call in ill or go home early on sick leave. Since they won't let you call in too stupid to work, or too tired to work, or too angry to work, or too depressed to work, or too fed up with the world to work, then you pretty much have to call in "sick." Fine, we all understand this.

But fifteen days a year?

The average number of absences per year per employee varies from industry to industry; retail stores have the highest, government and insurance are midrange, while public utilities, hospitals, and other offices are on the low end. Human service agencies, as near as I can tell, are below the average of about eleven days per year nationwide. In my own agency, we consider more than eight days of sick leave use per year above company and industry averages and worth looking into.

The average age of your staff plays into these statistics (the older the staff the more chronic, life-style type illnesses will have caught up to them) but a good rule of thumb is that, excepting unusual, long-term illnesses, most staff should be absent from their jobs fewer than eight days a year, and the great majority will miss no more than one to three days. For a program goal (made up of high-priced clinicians) I strive for an average usage of four or five days a year. Barring a major surgery or serious illness, this is usually attainable.

Here's a typical problem detected by this simple leave report: John Doe seems to be sick a lot and others are having to cover for him in the program.

From your monthly or quarterly sick-leave report, you can see that John Doe has used six sick days between January 1 and March 31 (a three-month interval). Your hunch about excessive absenteeism has been confirmed. Projecting these figures ahead for the remaining nine months of the year, and at the current rate, John is going to considerably exceed the agency's average of eight days per twelve-month interval.

If you know John was sick with a virus for five days, then you've probably no need for action. But if he's been sick one day here, one day there, a couple of Fridays, then you and John may have a problem—especially if last year's report shows he was absent thirteen days.

Remembering the eighty/twenty rule (that 20 percent of the staff will use 80 percent of the sick leave—see chapter 12) you have just identified one of the 20 percenters. Now you can focus your efforts and take some action.

The Detailed Sick-Leave Report

We still have our mystery—the staffer who was missing two afternoons of work a month.

Once you have identified an employee whose absenteeism is excessive (and it is important to get projections from your first-level report about those employees likely to exceed your annualized average cutoff so that you can act promptly) then ask for a detailed report.

A detailed report (which you can do yourself) is simply a calendar marked with the specific days and times the employee was absent. This visual aid can be very enlightening.

Once you have the pattern of absences before you on a calendar, compare the days the staffer is ill against his obligations on those days. Consider the following:

- What are the staffer's obligations on the days he is gone? (It is amazing how often people get ill on the days they have the fewest obligations and how rarely people get ill on payday.) In my experience, when professional people helpers have a significant responsibility to perform, they will drag themselves off their deathbed to get the job done.
- Look for a pattern of every third Tuesday, every other Monday; Fridays? Since genuine illness is a random event, any sort of pattern may be a clue to abuse.
- Compare this year's sick use pattern with last year's. If there was excessive use in prior years, is the pattern the same or different?
- Single-day illnesses are relatively rare (most disabling viruses last two or more days) and a repeated pattern of one-day absenteeism suggests something other than true illness unless, of course, this is the sort of person who comes to work sick. Many hospitals and other health care agencies insist sick staff take sufficient time to get well and not come back to work so early as to spread whatever they've got around.

Non-illness Reasons Staff Use Sick Leave
- The husband's company doesn't allow time off when a child is ill; therefore, the mother who works for you must use her sick leave.

- The person is angry about something and has elected to get even by "skipping school." (Look for recent administrative changes, a new boss, or anything that has required a major readjustment in the staffer's work and may have negatively impacted his attitude.)
- A single incident may have frightened the employee (an assault, a threat, a blowup with a client that has not been resolved, etc.).
- An outside job. If a staffer has a second job, he may have to skip work at your shop from time to time to keep it.
- Depending on your point of view, the Bourbon Flu. Whether disease or bad habit, missing work due to hangovers will often show up in a pattern of missed Mondays. But not necessarily. Since many alcoholics plan their drunks, study the staffer's obligations on the days he is absent. The fewer the obligations, the easier it will be to have "just one more."

There are many other reasons people use and abuse sick leave when they are not sick. Negative feelings toward the agency, an attitude of entitlement ("I deserve three mental health days a year even if this crummy outfit doesn't think so"), personal errands that have to be run, family crises, and a host of others. And while I am not suggesting that all use of sick leave be brought to a halt, I am suggesting that when it is known by staff that sick leave is being abused by some employees, allowing it to continue unchecked is both demoralizing and contagious. If high absenteeism becomes institutionalized, the loss of effectiveness and efficiency to the agency and clients can be staggering.

Now back to the Case of the Missing Staffer.

After a careful analysis of the staffer's pattern of missed afternoons (two per month, the same afternoon) I called his supervisor in for a chat.

"What is Bill doing Tuesday afternoons?"

"Hummm. Let's see. Oh, he runs a group with Carla. A depression group."

"Every other week?"

"Yes. The group only meets twice a month."

"Anything going on between Bill and Carla?" I asked.

"I don't think so."

"Didn't they go to a conference together a couple of months ago? I remember approving some travel for them."

"Yes. Come to think of it, they've been acting a little odd since they got back."

(Neither Carla nor Bill was married, but from my general search operator at the front desk the priority traffic was that their brief out-of-office affair had crashed in flames.)

"Why don't you bring up the subject individually with Bill and Carla?" I said. "I think they'll level with you."

As it turned out, the rumor mill (read: intelligence sources) were right: Bill and Carla's office romance had ended in a huge fight. Except when absolutely necessary, they were barely speaking to one another. Bill, a solid professional and the dumpee, had chosen to be "ill" on afternoons they led the group together rather than burden the clients with his difficult-to-hide feelings. A simple intervention and a reassignment of duties solved the problem.

Appointment Books

In case you do not have a computerized data system to capture staff activities, caseload size, numbers of billable events per week, etc., the week-at-a-glance appointment book is probably your best source of information about how and where the staff are spending their time.

Assuming they have one, once you get the staff past the idea that you need to see their appointment book to help them plan their time (some may resist you) you can quickly appraise the following:

- number of clients scheduled each week
- the hours of the day clients are scheduled
- the kinds and numbers of meetings they attend
- how many hours they have set aside for paperwork and phone calls
- how, generally, they have set up their week's work

To help staff balance out their duties so that they have sufficient time to handle emergencies, return phone calls, and otherwise manage their time effectively, the appointment book can be a very useful management tool. Again, you get a visual aid and a "feel" for how their work is organized.

Caseload Data

While comprehensive caseload data is best gotten with the aid of computers and a daily submission of service data by staff, on even a low budget you should be able to keep track of the following by simply having each staff person keep a ledger or list of his active clients. Set up in columns on a single piece of lined paper, the database can include:

- client name and phone number
- total active cases (keep a running total in upper right-hand corner)
- date of intake (to get at length of stay)
- diagnosis for each case
- number of visits to date (keep track with hatch marks)
- modality of service (individual, group, marital, etc.)

You can keep track of other things for clinical supervisory matters, but at least the above gives you and your staff person a ready handle on how many, what kind, how long, and how often she is seeing clients. Also, in the event the staffer gets sick or is going to be gone even for a day, the person covering for her will find a copy of this caseload information most helpful—especially since medical records seldom track clients by the therapist assigned.

It is a simple operation to keep a copy of all of these one-page caseload data sheets from your staff, sum up the numbers of clients seen by each and get a quick total of active cases for your program; e.g., five therapists with twenty-five active clients each equals a caseload of 125.

By summing the types of diagnoses or problems your staff work with, you can quickly define your most typical client or clients. Are most depressed? Schizophrenic? Families in crises? What?

Then if you add the number of client hours scheduled (from their appointment books) and subtract the nonclient nondirect service hours (training, supervision, administrative meetings, no shows, etc.) you will arrive at a figure which constitutes the total available hours your staff have for direct or billable service.

With available hours for service in one hand, caseload size, type of service, and description of the typical client in the other (and some idea of how long people stay in your service), it is a quick step to answer many of the questions program managers are asked:

- How many people do you see in your service?
- What kind of people do you serve?
- What sort of problems do these people have?
- How many clients is each staff responsible for?
- What kind of treatment do they get?
- How much time do your staff have to really work with clients?

In my own view, if a manager can answer these few questions any time I ask them, I'm satisfied she has a pretty good idea of how and what is going on in her department, at least as regards efficiency.

The Charting-Error Report

This one takes a little time and costs a little money. But unless you are one of the few organizations who are not monitored by an outside regulatory agency, you should find some sort of charting-error report invaluable to your monitoring responsibilities.

This is a simple report and usually consists of the following data: name of staff person reviewed, how many charts were examined for completeness, percent of charts found imperfect, up-to-date condition, and a listing of the errors found.

It is a good idea to carefully establish standards for what represents a good chart (involving staff in the process), separate critical chart errors from casual errors (medication order missing vs. the wrong date for a progress note), and tally only the critical errors in determining if a chart meets criteria.

Using a 5 or 10 percent random sampling procedure, a small group of clinical staff led by medical records (or whoever is in charge of your records keeping), you should be able to accomplish the following important functions:

- have charts in a perpetual state of readiness for auditors and inspectors
- avoid charges of fraud for wrongful billing of services that have been rendered but have not been documented in the chart
- earn a reputation as a conscientious agency who takes its responsibilities seriously
- identify those staff who repeatedly fail to keep their charts in order (take these to task) and, more importantly, identify those staff who do a good job (reinforce these folks)
- keep your medical records staff happy and, more importantly, keep your boss looking good
- stop all the haranguing about paperwork that may be going on in your agency; by setting up a routine chart check and routine report to you, you should put a stop to the whiny old question, "Why do we have to do all this stuff anyway?"

In spite of how staff may feel about doing paperwork, it is much more than a necessary evil. With client welfare as the guiding principal, it is the client who deserves and has a right to good paperwork, legible notes, thorough written evaluations, timely correspondence on their behalf, and a complete, accurate, up-to-date chart that can be read by anyone in case of an emergency. At least for me, 100 percent accuracy in client charting is not a pie-in-the-sky goal, it is something quite attainable and something that should be expected. Period.

As an aside, I will tolerate a bit of sloppy paperwork for a period of a few weeks while a new staff person is learning the ropes. But once he's reached freeway speed, I expect the paperwork to be essentially perfect. If it doesn't get near perfect with some help, encouragement, and feedback (and unless the person has some sort of legitimate handicap), then one of us is going to start looking for a job. And it isn't going to be me.

Bottom line: If, as a manager, you are willing to put up with poor paperwork and sloppy charting because you don't think it is all that important to the work of your agency then, believe me, you will get it. Lots of it.

Finally, in terms of low-budget tools and especially since training has become a major part of any professional's life, some system needs to be in place to keep track of staff training. Some staff get too much training, others not enough. As a manager in our field, I would suggest you not leave the amount, type, or record keeping of training entirely up to your staff.

Have them keep track of it in a special file, on their appointment books, or in their personnel file . . . , but have them keep track. Check their training status at least quarterly. Otherwise you will find folks coming at you with urgent and usually expensive training requests to keep some license or certification. Or you may have auditors frowning because half your people didn't get sufficient training hours to pass some review.

High-Budget Management Tools

There are not that many high-budget management tools. Excepting a graduate degree in an appropriate area and twenty years of experience, the most expensive management tool any agency can purchase is a good computer and the appropriate softwear.

I will assume that the reader is no longer struggling with whether computers should or should not be admitted into the human services field. They're here. They may not be perfect, but they are here. And they are here to stay.

In my view (and I fought many a bloody battle during the Invasion of the Body Counters some years back), a manager who is not computer savvy is never going to be all the manager she can be. Computers store, massage, treat, and deliver information that is critical not only to daily operations but, in the long run, the mission and purpose of the agency. You must, somehow come to trust and, yeah! even love your computer.

Enough of sermonette.

In a high-budget operation, a high-quality, computer-based information system can provide the manager with any and all of the following:

- number of intakes per month
- number of terminations/discharges per month
- total active caseload by therapist/by program
- total clients served during report interval
- median length of stay by therapist/by program
- available staff hours
- percent of direct service hours
- percentage of appointments kept (no-show rate)
- treatment hours per client per month
- caseload per full-time equivalent
- cost of treatment per client, by modality, episode, program, etc.
- gain or loss per treatment hour or modality
- average daily attendance in a program
- bed day utilization per report interval

The list goes on and on. Not only can program descriptive data be made available, even simple research questions can be asked and answered.

If you have budget responsibilities, then even more data may be available to you—spreadsheets, cost analyses, expenditure projections, and the like. If you can get budget/cost information tied to your client/caseload data, so much the better.

But maybe the most important functions the computer can serve are to permit the following:

- monthly monitoring figures for managers and staff to see if they are reaching program goals (key indicators of productivity)
- quarterly, semiannual, and yearly figures for the same purpose
- agency-wide data to satisfy contract requirements of funding agencies
- quick answers to knotty questions; e.g., is therapist A keeping clients too long (average length of stay greater than for the other staff)? is therapist B doing something in session in her intake interviews that results in a 30 percent no-show rate for second appointments? when therapist C says he

gets all the really depressed and suicidal people is he accurate, or just feeling stressed out?

Depending on the sophistication of the system, the possibilities are essentially limitless. Even more important than the valuable routine reports to managers is the potential for special reports. A good system can answer important questions about utilization, costs, allocation of resources, caseload ratios, treatment outcomes, and many many other matters of critical importance to the operation of the agency.

But this chapter is not the place to detail the possibilities of the computer age as it applies to the delivery of human services, especially since by the time this book is published things will have advanced even more. But together with developing clinical applications of computers—psychological testing, diagnostic questionnaires, etc.—the manager needs to be ready, willing, and able to take advantage of these marvelous tools.

One word of caution.

If you do not yet have computers at your command and you are about to bring them on line, be prepared for resistance from some clinical staff about their utilization and purpose. Invasion of privacy. Big Brotherism. Seemingly "unnecessary" forms to fill out. Performance monitoring so that you can fire slackers? Burdens. Burdens. Burdens. My advice? Put up with it, move ahead, and make sure you help staff see the relevance of the data and the system.

Here are a few things that can help staff come to at least respect computers.

- Use no computer data to make decisions unless you, personally, are *absolutely* certain the data are *absolutely* accurate.
- Let staff keep their own data for a while, parallel with bringing the computer on line. When they are convinced the system is accurate and reliable, only then ask them to lay down their pencils.
- Reduce staff nuisance work by keeping track of their training, providng them an up-to-date caseload picture any time they ask for one, and show them how the computer can give

them a better handle on things like their no-show rate, collections, or whatever is pertinent to their particular job.

- Get a computer with a modem that will allow you to conduct literature searches for the staff on their request.
- Graph relevant data. Productivity, intakes per month, census figures, whatever . . . visual aids sell better than raw columns of numbers.
- Be prepared to be challenged, and encourage it. Our program manager responsible for staff data has a standing bet: If your numbers are correct and his are incorrect, he will buy you a Coke. He hasn't bought many Cokes.

Lastly, if a computer can't help the line staff, it isn't much of a system and will most assuredly generate more enemies than friends.

Whatever questions your computer-based intelligence system answers for you, it should help you answer the big one: Who, what, and where do I need to spend my management time today?

Other high-budget management tools include management-training seminars, staff-planning days, building a management library, hiring consultants, and providing specific, targeted (and usually expensive) training to key staff to increase their skill and knowledge levels about such things as organizational analysis, financial management, program evaluation, fund-raising, board building, community relations, grant writing, working with the mass media, public speaking, and a host of other things top managers must eventually learn to do.

But since this book is targeted more at the middle manager, I'll leave these subjects to those better informed than myself. My point, though, is that while every manager needs some simple, low-cost tools with which to work (a hammer and some nails), there is no real end to the process of growth and development for the manager. Friends of mine have found management so interesting they have gone back to school to earn MBAs or Masters in Public Administration. Others have attended staff colleges sponsored by the National Institute of Mental Health and still others have earned special certificates to better qualify them to do their jobs.

In summary, management is a career, not just a set of skills you can get from a book like this. You may be able to get along with only a hammer and nails today, but if you have a chance to pick up a saw and a level and a screwdriver, and can learn a little about plumbing and wiring and insulation, one day you may be able to build the whole house.

6

Delegation

Mark Twain once wrote, "To be good is noble, but to teach others how to be good is nobler . . . and much less trouble." My job in this chapter is to help you help others to be nobler. If you happen to save yourself a ton of time, a pile of trouble, get your job done better, and help your agency achieve its mission in an effective and efficient manner, then so much the better.

As you will learn in the chapter on time management, the greatest time saver ever built is the manager who delegates well. A critical skill, here are some things delegation is:

- entrusting authority in someone else to act as your agent or representative
- giving specific decision-making power to someone else, usually in a specified area for a specified time period
- within certain boundaries, leaving someone in charge of your job, with all its attendant obligations and responsibilities

In my view, the basic notion underlying delegation is an act of trust—but an act of trust that requires your best judgment. It is not enough to delegate an important job to someone and then, when they botch it, retreat to the position that, after all, "I gave Harry that job and he blew it."

Wrong. You blew it. If you asked Harry to do a job for which he was neither trained nor sufficiently experienced, then you, as the person who told Harry to do it, are the responsible party. Harry just did what he was told. In the art of delegation, the manager's job is simple; you always pick the right person for the right job.

In its simplest terms, delegation means to get your work done through others by giving them the *right* to make decisions for you. For example, asking a staff person to take something down to the Xerox room and run off a few copies for you is not delegation; delegation is asking that same staff person to *decide* which of all the papers in a given pile should be copied, who should get those copies, and then to go ahead and route the material. In the first instance your basic robot will do, in the second case you will need the help of a "thinking" human being.

I might note here that staff are very much aware of when they are being asked to "play robot" and when they are being asked to stand in your stead. While the first request is a chore, the second is a privilege, and it is the wise manager who can make one into the other.

Here are some things delegation is not:

- giving someone all of the responsibility and none of the authority
- asking someone to interview a job applicant and report his impressions back to you so that, now that you have his observations, you can interview the same applicant and make up your own mind. (If you were not allowing the staff person to make the decision to hire—and unless you only wanted some preliminary data—why bother having him conduct the interview?)
- asking someone to conduct a clinical staff meeting in your presence and then, throughout the meeting, asking all the questions yourself, directing the topics of discussion, changing the agenda, and otherwise running the show.
- assigning a report to be written and then, when the report comes back, rewriting the whole thing in your own inimitable style.
- asking someone to "take over" while you're gone for a few days and, upon your return, dressing down your subordinate for approving a staffer to take educational leave to

attend a seminar you feel (now that you've seen the bro-
chure) was not worth the price of admission.
- giving a staffer the responsibility to spend the company's
money, but only if those expenditures meet with your approval . . . approval you will consider giving sometime after
the checks clear the bank.
- sending a staffer to another agency to complete a consultation but, just to be on the safe side, tagging along to
"help out."
- giving a staffer the job of writing up a project at which,
after you see the first rough draft, you throw up your
hands and reassign it to someone else.

One common thread running through most of these apparent acts of delegation is this: THE WORK IS BEING DONE TWICE.
Anytime you do the same job with two different people, you are
a failed delegator and a poor manager. Do the work of one
person with three people (three times over) and someone
should be hanged (figuratively speaking, of course—although,
given my sentiments about wasting time, I'd help find a rope).
Another common thread running through these examples is
that, despite what the delegator may have said, he never really
delegated anything. You can't ask a staffer to use his own head
to make decisions while you're gone, and then come back and
beat him up for using his own head.

Why Delegate?
There are three major reasons a manager must learn to
delegate. First, it is presumed that since she is a creative problem solver, the agency needs her valuable ideas to solve its most
pressing problems. To have time to solve the problem of how to
drain the swamp, the manager must be able to assign others to
fight the alligators. Delegation of work means more time for the
manager to work on the right tasks. One of the best pieces of
managerial advice I ever received was as follows: "We don't
want you to waste time doing anything you can hire someone
else to do." And, as long as the money held out, that is what I
did.
Second, unless you delegate some of your work to your staff,

you will stunt their growth. They will not learn and stretch to higher and higher standards of performance. It is crucial to your agency that when you are sick or unavailable, your job continues to get done. But to have someone there to fill in for you, you first have to train them up, get them comfortable with your functions and responsibilities, and communicate to them that you know they can do your job just fine. The only way to achieve this is through delegation.

Third, delegation forces you to become organized. To see to it that a complicated set of tasks get accomplished, you must pick the people for the jobs, set deadlines, monitor progress, and otherwise orchestrate the project. This is, after all, why they call us managers.

Resisting Delegation

There is an old saw in our culture that goes, "If you want a job done right, you have to do it yourself." Sometimes this is true, but often it is a cover for the person who cannot, for some reason, relinquish control, authority, and the right to make decisions to those who work for him. This may be a fine attitude if you are a diamond cutter and about to split a five-million-dollar stone, but it is simply an unacceptable position for most managers to assume.

In my experience, managers who have trouble delegating properly have some or all of the following characteristics in common:

- They may foster dependency, as in, "Don't you worry about a thing, dear, I'm the boss and I'll take care of it. Here, let me do that for you. . . ."
- They may have a high need for control. Apparently operating from the premise that they are the Great I-AM and know everything about everything, they will not let those who work for them do that for which they are perfectly trained, qualified, and paid. This is the supervisor who looks over shoulders for a living, must redo the work of his staff, and seems constitutionally unable to trust anyone to do anything right.
- They may be too passive and have a fear of imposing on

others, as in, "Oh, gosh . . . , gee . . . , I wonder if I could ask you to . . . , no, no, you look terribly busy. Never mind. I'll come back later." Managers who are too nice to ask their staff to help them get their job done need some backbone building from their own boss. Managers must get their work done through their staffs, otherwise why bother having managers at all?

- They may worry a subordinate will do his job better than they are doing it. Fearing an unfavorable comparison, they keep their boss deluded and needy of them by never giving those below them a chance to shine through the fog they have created. By never giving staff a challenging job to complete, an opportunity to develop a special project, or give a report to the board, or even to take fair credit for a good idea, such managers may keep their jobs, but they will fail their agencies.

In my experience, this latter sort of person is too insecure about his own skills, adequacy, and job tenure to be an effective manager—sometimes mean-spirited and destructive of his staff into the bargain. It is always the mission of the agency that suffers in the long run.

A final point. Every agency needs *all* the talents of *all* its staff. To get everyone's talents working for the welfare of clients, managers must delegate, share responsibility, groom others for leadership, and otherwise bring out the best in everyone who works for them.

The Test for Indispensability
Pardon a slip from the epigrammatic pen: While it is nice to be told you are indispensable; it is quite another thing to *believe* you are.

Like a lot of psychologists, I have always wanted to invent my own psychological test—you know, one with high reliability, perfect validity, and one that would become an indispensable tool in the assessment of human behavior, thus making me rich and famous. Well, the best I've been able to do is swipe what I will herewith call the Test for Indispensability.

This test (whose origins I do not know) was apparently developed especially for those managers who do not know how to delegate and who, as a result, believe themselves to be indispensable. Here is how I came to steal this test.

Many years ago an alcohol counselor who worked for me dropped by my office and asked me if I wanted to go to lunch. I said, sorry, I was too busy for lunch. (Back in those days I thought a good manager spent his lunch hours humped over a desk with little beads of sweat popping out of his brow while he wrestled with problems of historic moment and dire consequence, preferably with his office door propped open so that staff less critical to the operation could see that the Main Man was still slaving away while they, God bless them, were going out for a relaxing lunch.)

"Too busy, eh?" asked Sheldon.

"Yes," I said, offended that he apparently could not see the sweat dripping from my troubled brow.

"Have you passed the test for indispensability?" he asked.

"Huh?" I said. "What test is that?"

"Well," Sheldon said, "if you are truly indispensable and you can pass this test, then you should stay right there at your desk and work through the lunch hour . . . otherwise you have to come to lunch with me."

"So what's this test?"

He began, "You take a bucket and fill it to the rim with water. Then you stick your hand down into the water all the way up to your wristwatch. Then you quickly pull your hand back out of the water. If the water doesn't rush back in and there is a hand-shaped hollow still in the water, then you are truly indispensable and should stay here and work."

I forgot where and what we had for lunch that day, but I never forgot the lesson. Having failed the Test of Indispensability, I subsequently promoted Sheldon to a supervisory job so that he could spend a few of his lunch hours doing some of my work. Managers may be a lot of things, but dumb ain't one of them.

Delegation Made Simple

Once you've examined and gotten past any internal resistance to delegating some of your work to others, *what* to delegate becomes a key question. And while you may feel a bit uneasy about asking someone to do a job you are not really sure he can do, delegation means taking risks—calculated risks. Unfortunately, you will never know if a staffer can do something until you give him a chance. As they say, no guts, no gain.

Here are some tips I think are helpful to the process:

- Considering the task at hand, ask yourself: What's the worst that can happen? If the worst that can happen is that the staffer turns in a poor project, or embarrasses herself making a presentation, or lets a meeting deteriorate into a shouting match, then, depending on how important you judge these outcomes to be, you can make your decision.

Note: If the worst possible outcome is clearly unacceptable, then don't delegate the responsibility, task, or decision—do it yourself.

- If the worst that can happen is still within a range of acceptable outcomes, then make the assignment as follows: give clear instructions, define the result you want, set a timetable, and (this is important) let the staffer know you are available for questions and consultation.
- Convey the impression that you are confident the job will be done right. In a word, don't hover, fret, or stand around wringing your hands. You can, however, wring your hands in the privacy of your office, or even pace if you like. The main thing is to exude complete confidence to the staffer you are delegating to, even though you may have reservations.
- Since you've told the staffer to come to you with questions or concerns, don't get antsy and check in every couple of minutes to see how things are going. As a rule, staff will take longer to do one of your jobs than it takes you to do it. Don't crowd, don't step in and finish the job yourself, and don't get upset if it isn't done precisely on time.
- Whatever else you do, and as long as the job is done within your range of reasonable outcomes, *do not* redo the job. Nothing will devastate a staff person's sense of accomplish-

ment or tender ego-investment quicker than stepping in, tossing their work in the trash, and redoing the whole thing yourself.

- Even if you are not all that pleased with the job, delay your criticism a bit and see, in fact, how things turn out. You may discover that despite your high standards, your subordinate's solution to a problem was just fine—even though, of course, it lacked the benefit of your genius touch.
- If you are delegating to a new employee or the task is a long and arduous one, offer to check in. You don't want someone to flounder unnecessarily.
- Give credit and praise where it is earned; privately is okay, publicly is best. When you brag publicly about staffers for a job well done, they tend to puff up to about twice their natural size and their smiles last about two weeks.
- When everything goes wrong that can go wrong, accept the blame, quickly and completely.

Some Final Thoughts

Whatever you may think about delegating work to others, it is important to remember that despite how important you are to the organization (and I have no doubt that you are), you are never so important that the agency should not be able to get along without you. No one manager should ever be so critical to an operation that the mission (or even the welfare of a single client) is endangered if that manager should suddenly drop dead.

Henry Ford, the founder of the Ford empire, did not believe in the concept of managers or managerial teams. He knew how to build cars and he, by damn, would make all the decisions. Mr. Ford did this very well, but he delegated very little, especially in terms of rights and powers to make decisions. Then one day he died. Thrown into chaos because no one had experience with decision making or the judicious use of power or how to delegate the work, the Ford Motor Company almost died with him. It wasn't until his grandson, Edsel Ford, took over and developed a management team that the Ford Motor Company was able to again be competitive in the marketplace.

You may not be the chief executive officer of a major corporation, but your responsibilities to your agency, your boss, your staff, and clients are not diminished by the comparison. As a manager you must do everything you can to see to it that the best decisions are made where and when they will do the most good.

In my experience, it is the people below us who are working daily with the daily problems who often have best solutions. Not every time, but many times. Unless we give them permission to tackle the problems on their own, the right to decide what to do and how to do it, and the authority to act, we will never know what they might have contributed to the success of the mission.

7

Hiring

One of the fun parts about being a manager is offering people a job. Few things are more valued in our culture than steady employment and nothing so raises a person's self-esteem as getting that all-important phone call. In terms of good news, I'd rank landing a job right up there with the birth of a child or graduating from college—which is why, if it becomes necessary, it can be so difficult to fire that same person some months or years later. Because terminating an employee can be so traumatic, I've devoted an entire chapter to the subject.

Since good people are the key to the success of any business or service organization, a manager has to learn to hire (and fire) well. In fact, if you do this job poorly, the mission of your agency is jeopardized. When you consider that somewhere between 80 and 90 percent of your organization's entire budget is devoted to salaries and benefits, you might think of hiring and maintaining your work force as *the* most important job you do, at least when it comes to spending the company's money. So let's begin with the fun part.

As a general hiring philosophy, I'd like to suggest that you only consider hiring people smarter than yourself. By smarter, I mean people who know the job you are asking them to do better than you do. I'm not talking about those professionals in our field who hold certain kinds of licenses to do certain things that you, personally, are not licensed to do, I'm talking about hiring people who are, in experience, training, and skill, better at some things than you are. In a word, I'm talking about hiring excellence.

To put together an excellent staff (and unless you are the most highly trained clinician or counselor in the world and can do everything better than everybody else), you will need to hire people more skilled than yourself. To do this, you must set aside your ego, think of the mission, and realize that, as a manager, your star only shines though the work of the people who work for you.

The dynamic CEO for whom I have worked the majority of my professional career has repeatedly said, "Whenever others praise me and the work this agency does, they rarely forget to mention what a terrific staff I have. That, of course, is no accident."

At the other extreme, I have seen some otherwise very capable managers repeatedly surround themselves with inadequate staff for reasons, I can only guess, that have to do with the idea that they will somehow look good by comparison. Or maybe they feel threatened by highly qualified supervisees. I don't know. But I do know that if you surround yourself with people less able than yourself, the mission you've undertaken will suffer, your burdens as a manager will be heavy, and the clients you serve will not get the best possible help available. Enough philosophy.

Here, in no order of importance, are my rules and tips to good hiring.

1. Don't be in a hurry. Social service agencies are not producing war materials or fuel for an already-scheduled space launch, so take the time you need to find the right people. Search locally first, then in nearby cities, then in nearby states. Since most positions don't warrant moving expenses, the less distance the new employee has to travel the better.

2. Unless you've the wisdom of Job, don't make the decision to hire entirely by yourself. In this, the recruiting and thinking phase, ask yourself these questions: "What sort of person, specifically, do I need and want? What skills does this person need to have to improve my department? How much of my job can this person do better than I can?"

This last question is the most difficult to answer, partly because it depends on whether or not you also carry clinical or counseling responsibilities. But if you can answer it honestly (and can find that person who can do part of your work better than you) then your job will be easier and you will be free to do other things.

Once you know the sort of person you need and have a job description in hand, invite key staff on the team to share in the résumé reviewing and the interviews. But don't put the applicant through a huge "team interview" composed of six, or eight, or ten staffers. A job interview should produce a little anxiety, but not a panic attack.

If you've got a personnel officer, be sure she is involved in the process from the beginning. Know the Equal Employment Opportunity Commission rules governing what you can and cannot ask of an applicant during an interview. Personnel can help keep you and your agency from embarassing yourselves by making sure your job interview is a perfectly legal one. If you don't know these laws, learn them.

When it comes to hiring, three heads (one of whom knows what a legal interview is) are always better than one. Also, it helps to gain the support of your staff when selecting a new member to the team, even though you may have to make the final decision.

3. Check résumés carefully. Personnel experts know that about 20 percent of the experience reported by job applicants is bogus, i.e., creative fiction. People will report two full years of experience when, in fact, they were only employed for one year and seven months. "Full-time" jobs were only part-time, etc. Since years of experience often translate to the level of the starting salary, it is critical to get the numbers right the first time around—otherwise you and the employee are off on the wrong foot and an inequity has been established that can, if discovered later, cause no end of complaining, diminished morale, and all-round suffering . . . , including your own for being sloppy to begin with.

Occasionally the mental health field is invaded by out-and-out impostors who masquerade as trained professionals. Having unmasked a few myself, here's the best way to catch them. First, *assume nothing!* Because the person last worked for a well-known agency may only mean that that agency never tumbled to the ruse. Next, call or write the registrars at the universities from which they claim to have matriculated. Registrars are familiar with these requests and will not refuse a legitimate inquiry for verification. No degree, no hire.

When it comes to spending the company's time and money, I can think of no better place to spend it than in the thorough review required to make a fair yet careful assessment of a potential employee's background.

4. Although not easy to determine, try to hire people without obvious problems. This may seem a rather stupid observation, but I have been amazed at how often trained clinicians seem to make this mistake. It is as if when they begin a job interview their usually good clinical nose goes on the blink.

Also, since terminated employees are successfully suing past employers for damaging their character and job prospects by writing candid and negative letters of reference to future employers, it is increasingly difficult to get the inside dope on someone's past employment problems. Still, you must try. A phone call with assurances that the respondent's remarks are "strictly confidential" will net the quickest, most honest information.

5. Sometime during the interview, ask the question, "What sorts of ethical problems have you encountered in your past work and how have you handled these?" This question may net you important information about the character of your interviewee or, if you're lucky, may trigger a revelation about a personal ethical violation. Failure to ask this question may lead you to hire someone whose character flaws are already a matter of public record in another state—a revelation that can be very embarrassing when your boss or governing board or some attorney or some newspaper reporter asks you, "You mean you didn't know this man was a sex offender?"

6. A good way to get a feel for the person's clinical work is to ask the following question (one I learned to ask as a board examiner while licensing psychologists): "Could you take a case from recent experience and tell me (us) how the person was referred, how you sized up the problem, and what sort of treatment plan you carried out?"

Better than any other question, the answers you get should tell you at least the following: how the person presents a case (e.g., for a staffing), how the person "thinks" about clinical problems, and what, in theory and practice, does this person actually do with clients. Also, the question opens up the interview to allow you to investigate other areas; formal theoretical orientation, types of clients she has worked with, and so forth.

(I have, by the way, found a job applicant's theoretical orientation to therapy practically noncontributory to the decision to hire—rigid psychoanalysts and rabid behaviorists notwithstanding.)

7. Try to assess willingness and ability to learn and work. If the interviewee scores high on these, you can't go too far wrong. You might also consider this question: While this candidate has the training and credentials to do this job, *will* he do it? When it comes to actual performance after the hiring is done, there is sometimes a great deal of difference between *can* and *will*.

A friend of mine hires frontline counseling and case manager staff otherwise qualified by training and experience if they meet three simple criteria: good affect, good attitude, and a demonstrated willingness to learn. He argues that since he must teach them the details of what they need to know anyway (and as long as they are not clinically depressed, overtly hostile, or clearly passive/aggressive) their positive attitude will lead to good integration on his team. "Always hire bright, happy people," he says. It seems to work well for him.

The only thing I would add to his list, and although it's probably impossible to assess in a few minutes, would be character. With staff of good character, the manager has little need of rule making or potions to help him sleep. I believe it was the army that taught me rules and regulations are only written to govern the stupid, the crooked, and the lazy.

8. Keep in mind that having been fired from a job is sometimes a positive recommendation. I can think of several institutions in our field where it would have been nothing short of an honor to have been dismissed for cause.

9. If you are having trouble finding people locally, try advertising in appropriate journals or, always much faster, in local

newspapers in adjoining states. Even better, buy newspaper advertising in states where social and mental health services are undergoing major cutbacks. Since the rule is that the best people leave such states earlier than the rest (they're not the best because they're dumb), you can sometimes land some very good folks by outreaching them.

Of course if you are searching for high-priced people (psychiatrists, a medical or executive director, clinical psychologists, etc.) then, since these people don't look for jobs in the want ads of their local papers, you will have to buy space in the appropriate journals, trade magazines, or in-house newsletters. Some of the professional publications can take months to reach their readerships, so as soon as you know you're going to have an opening and can't snare some local talent, start the search the next day.

10. In case you can't find someone right away it is, in my view, far better to leave a position unfilled than to fill it with the wrong person. If you or a member of the interview team has grave misgivings about someone, *pay attention to these gut feelings*. If, after the interview is over and the discussion leads to a split decision because someone feels strongly negative, you can always schedule another interview with the same person to clear things up, check more thoroughly into the person's references, extend your search to new prospects, or do whatever is necessary to reach a consensus decision.

Because some jobs are more critical than others, a key position may have to go unfilled for months. When this happens, be sure you've advertised well, are paying enough to get the kind and caliber of person you want and need, and, finally, that no one on the interview team is sabotaging the process for reasons only they could best explain.

I might note that in my experience, people-helping agencies tend not to spend enough money where it counts . . . on key personnel. Keep your strongest people by paying them what they're worth and a host of other problems will simply disappear. Underpay your most important players and, if they're as good as they should be, someone else will be trying to lure them away.

It may help to be a little paranoid in this respect and to think of your best staff as frequently getting offers in the mail. Because the truth is, there aren't all that many blue-chip professionals around and, like it or not, you are always competing with other employers for their services—even after they've signed on with your agency. You'd be surprised how much agency loyalty you can buy if the price is right. Like the old manager said, "You can't afford to be stupid."

Here are some quick tips for the job interview itself:

- Put them at ease, then work them over. Try not to end an interview with unasked questions still on your mind.
- Ask the same questions of everyone. Consistency of inquiries is the key to a legal interview and the best way to avoid accusations of unfair hiring practices.
- Don't talk too much.
- Use more open-ended questions than closed-ended ones.
- Don't hesitate to probe.
- Try to imagine how the prospect will fit into your agency's social and power structure.
- Find out why the applicant wants to do this particular job in your particular agency.
- Make sure the applicant knows exactly what sort of job she is applying for. Be specific as to description of duties, details, typical day, etc.
- Don't be shy about discussing the *M* word. Money may not be everything, but for most of us it is considerably ahead of whatever is in third place. The applicant will be hesitant to say the *M* word, you shouldn't.
- Never apologize for the salary you can offer. (If you decide to hire the person, why start him off with the idea that he's worth more than you can afford?)
- Know your benefit package inside and out. A strong benefit package may be one of your best draws.
- Always follow up the interview with feedback to the interviewee. Whatever excuse you use if you choose not to hire the person ("Another applicant was more qualified," etc.), be kind and cordial. However you put it, the applicant was

rejected and should be let down easily. Besides, you never know when you may wish to hire this person for another job at another time.

Hiring may be easier than firing, but if you make a serious mistake at the outset you will, unfortunately, get an opportunity to correct it, sometimes sooner rather than later. In the meantime you have wasted valuable time and done nothing for your reputation as a manager.

One final note. Whatever you do, take cautionary heed of any therapeutic twinges that occur during a job interview—it may mean the applicant needs therapy, not a job. Too much sympathy felt for an applicant stumbling through the interview, empathetic urges to take this person under your wing, or the passing thought that "Gee, he seems a little reckless, but with good supervision and a little time his judgment should improve"* are only a few of the warning signs that you may be on the verge of doing something you will later regret.

Having made this mistake a few times myself, I suggest that when hiring staff you keep the following slip of the epigrammatic pen in mind: "We are operating a service business here, not a sheltered workshop."

*Just between us chickens, I have yet to see a case of poor judgment improve—on its own, either in response to the most vigorous applications of supervision, or with the help of all the king's horses and all the king's men.

8

Firing

Because our training is to always be helpful, kind, understanding, and empathetic, letting an employee go is clearly the toughest job a people-helper manager ever undertakes. As a result, firing is often done poorly . . . if at all.

I say "if at all" because in my experience there are very few agencies or institutions in our field that could not benefit greatly from the selective termination of one or more of the people presently on the payroll of the organization. This observation probably does not apply to your particular organization, but I will wager it applies to an organization you know about and, surely, to one you once worked for.

Before we get to the things you can do short of firing someone, let's take a quick look at the reasons you have not taken more definitive action with respect to that certain supervisee—you know, the one you've been worrying about, the one you've talked over with your spouse, the one that's making the whole department look bad.

First, if you're the one who hired this person, you're going to have to admit that you made a mistake. None of us likes to admit making a bad call, especially if it's a management decision. Relying heavily on denial, we go on covering for this employee, defending him to others, and allowing his poor performance or negative attitude to damage the work environment, the other staff and, in many cases, the clients and the quality of care.

Second, we pray for spontaneous recovery. We know we have

a problem employee and yet, because we are reluctant to act, we hope against hope that somehow he will shape up and our problem will magically go away. In my experience, this rarely happens. One of the unwritten rules of management is that if personnel problems are left alone, they tend to get worse.

Third, there's always the hope that in time this employee will find another job and move on. This might happen, but poor performers often know they are marginal and, as a result, will frequently cling to their jobs with great tenacity.

Ask yourself a question: Can my agency or I afford to wait for miracles?

If your answer is no, then I hope what follows will be helpful.

Before getting into the specifics of how to fire someone, let's take a moment to consider what else you can do.

EAPs

If your agency does not have an employee assistance program, it should. Since the great majority of employee problems are the direct result of ordinary life stresses (divorce, illness, death of a loved one, substance abuse, financial crises, personal or family problems, etc.) a great many worthwhile employees need not be forced to resign or be fired if, and only if, the management of the agency has a system whereby troubled people can get help.

The data are in on the usefulness of employee assistance programs and any social service, mental health, or people-helping agency that doesn't offer such a service to its employees isn't practicing what it preaches. Employees should be able to get help easily, quickly, confidentially, and inexpensively. Considering the costs of turnover (emotional and in real dollars), programs that help staff stay emotionally healthy and able to work are clearly one of the most important benefits in the employee's package and one of the best investments an agency can make.

A major positive side effect of a formal EAP for employees is the direct savings in time and turmoil when, as often happens, formal and informal treatment is going on among the staff within the agency. These sorts of goings-on may not happen at General Motors or IBM, but mental health types will often engage each other in therapy, sometimes at their places of business and on company time.

Unless the agency is willing to have its own staff as official clients, this practice can only lead to headaches, lost productivity, and role-blurring confusion—to say nothing of the possible liability problems for everyone involved. Having been through this particular war zone once or twice, I can safely say the better part of valor calls for a policy explicitly forbidding one staff member to treat another—at least on the agency's time and premises.

An EAP is one of the manager's most useful tools. With a deficiency report in one hand and a referral for professional help in the other, a disciplinary interview can stay focused where it should; on performance. If the employee raises issues of family or personal problems that have negatively affected her work, the manager has the answer—clean, neat, on target, and, best of all, humane and helpful.

If the employee resists a voluntary referral for help, the supervisor can then insist upon an evaluation for possible counseling as a condition for continuing employment. Even though staff rarely refuse a referral under these circumstances, it's best to be ready for any resistance and to know beforehand just what sort of final result you want. If what you want is to get the employee professional help (with or without his cooperation) then be prepared to go all the way.

Of course all staff should be formally made aware of the company's EAP at the time of hiring and, also, should be specifically encouraged to use it at any time they or a family member feels the need. We may not always be able to practice preventive mental health in our communities, but we should make every effort to do so with our staff.

I think it's important to remember that since a person's job is as meaningful and vital to his psyche as air and water are to his body, all reasonable efforts should be made to help an employee stay an employee, especially if he has successfully passed his probationary period or has been with the agency a long time. This may mean providing special training, extra supervision, or off-the-job counseling or legal assistance through an EAP. It may mean adjusting his schedule to accommodate day-care arrangements for his child, or helping her to secure transportation by sponsoring a car pool to and from the agency, or helping him to overcome any number of obstacles that lie in the way of getting to the job and getting it done the way you want it done.

For one example, it was only with the beginning of the industrial revolution that punctuality became so important to the employer. If a worker did not show up exactly on time, his absence from a complex, highly integrated organism composed of man and machine caused a work stoppage and, as a result, a direct loss in productivity and profit. If you weren't there to bolt on the left front fender in Mr. Ford's factory, the whole line stopped and Mr. Ford wasn't happy. But in mental health work I like to remind myself and others that we are not building Fords, launching rockets, or starting the trains between here and Chicago. We, of any of the service industries in America, should understand the concept of flextime and how to use it to accommodate not only ourselves but, more importantly, our clients.

Progressive Discipline

Progressive discipline is a nice, tidy concept that, if carried out in practice, leads to good results. Simply put, progressive discipline should help an employee improve his performance.

My definition of discipline involves getting and giving honest, critical feedback about the quality and quantity of one's work. It should not be perceived as step one to an eventual termination. Quite the opposite; it should lead to what you want—improved performance.

As the feedback becomes more and more formal and is clearly communicated, the employee should correct what needs correcting. If the employee does not get his or her act together, at least you have established a clear record of your efforts if it becomes necessary to terminate the person. But I will ask you to consider something else first.

It is my view that oftentimes staff end up being fired, not because they did not want to do the job they were given, but because their supervisor failed to clearly communicate what it was he wanted done and how. I think too often we assume people-helping staff are so self-actualized they don't need structure and direction. This can be a big mistake since (and here goes the epigrammatic pen again) one man's sense of freedom is another man's sense of abandonment. Be careful that as a manager, you actually *manage*.

Here is how progressive discipline works.

Jim is always a few minutes late for work and his first clients of the day have complained more than once.

First, you stop into Jim's office and say, "Jim, you've been getting in a little late and some clients have complained. Are you having a problem?"

Jim says no, and that he'll take care of it.

You go back to your office and make a note on your calendar that you spoke to Jim about his tardiness and on such and such a day, at such and such a time.

A week passes and Jim continues to be late, to the tune of two more complaints.

Second step: You call Jim to your office, set him down, and say this is the second time you've spoken to him about being late. You hear him out, tell him you're making *another* note about the problem and that you do not expect to have to speak to him again about it.

But Jim still doesn't get the word.

(It is sometimes useful, at this second feedback/discipline session, to have the employee sign a statement that they have been formally counseled about a problem. Such a record is very useful if worst comes to worst, but signing a document can feel a bit awkward for both you and the employee. Such a "statement of understanding" is less harsh than a job deficiency report [to be discussed in a moment], but however you choose to do it, you must let Jim know you are keeping a record of your corrective conversations with him.)

If you must speak to an employee a third time about the same problem, it is time to get serious. In terms of progressive discipline, you should be ready to complete a job deficiency report, or whatever you wish to call such a document.

The Job Deficiency Report

A job deficiency report is a formal statement of concern on the employer's part that the employee is not functioning up to expectation and that, if something doesn't change, much more serious action will have to be taken. In brief, you are saying to the person, "Because of x, y, or z, we're not sure you're going to make it here."

The job deficiency report should be specific as to problems and expectations for improvement—the more specific the better. The report should be dated and signed by both of you. It should always have a date and time certain for a formal review of the problem and, depending on how you see the problem, may include an extension of probation, or (for an old employee) a reversion to probationary status. If you feel the employee is having a personal problem that needs professional attention, now is the time to lean on him to get help or, in some cases, it may be time to insist he at least get an evaluation.

In a word, you *must* let the employee know that you consider the problem very serious and that if it doesn't get better, you will have to take the next step. The "next step" in progressive discipline is, generally, suspension or termination.

I might note here that while I take no pleasure in frightening the dickens out of an employee during one of these difficult corrective sessions, it is better to be perfectly honest about my intentions than to have to wonder (on the day I'm letting him go) if I was, in fact, candid in describing how serious I thought the problem was. I'm afraid many of us underestimate the motivational benefits of fear and, if fear is what it takes to get someone's attention that a change is needed or that he ought to get help, then I suppose I'm not above evoking it. (My drill sergeant in boot camp wasn't above it either and it seemed to work pretty well for him.)

However you handle this phase of progressive discipline, what you don't want is the following reaction to your final decision: "Firing me!? For *what*!!!? I didn't think you were serious. You don't really mean you're letting me go!?"

Suspension with or without pay is an action you may wish to consider in lieu of termination. Like every other action though, it must be included as a procedural option in your personnel policies. While I have never personally used this option (and it has been available to me), my guess is that except in the rare case, anyone I would want to suspend for more than a day or two should probably be canned or, if his pride was still intact, he would have already resigned.

There are, however, times when you may need to undertake some sort of investigation of the employee's alleged actions and having the option of suspending them during this time can be a very useful one.

Preparation for the Termination Interview

Make no mistake about it, firing someone is probably the most serious management decision you can make. Do it wrong and you will live to regret botching it up. Do it right and you deserve to take yourself out for an expensive dinner. Let's take this step by step.

First, since most employers have a probationary period (usually the first six months), it is always much easier to terminate someone during this period if he is not working out. The company's personnel policies require a lesser standard for ending the relationship during this time and, since neither the employee nor the agency has made that great an investment in one another, this is clearly the best possible time to cut your losses and undo the mistake you made in hiring. The trouble is, most of us cross our fingers, pray for a miracle, and let this window of opportunity pass.

Question: As a highly trained professional who makes judgments about people for a living (including predictions as to ability to learn, change, adapt, and function), how is it that after six full months of observation, you still don't know if a new employee is going to work out?

According to a dear friend who is not a mental health professional, it's because, and I quote, "You guys are all so wishy-washy." I think she's right.

Therefore, a new hire should be carefully evaluated *throughout* her probationary period and, if found lacking in one or more critical areas (I'll get to these in a minute), then do both of you a favor and sever the relationship.

Problems, Serious and Most Serious

In our field, I see two primary problem areas that warrant swift disciplinary action, including termination. The most serious of these are what I like to call "hanging offenses."

A hanging offense is, as the lawyers say, a clear, cogent, and convincing case of poor judgment that may have resulted in damages to a client. Such acts are not simple acts of negligence but, rather, represent a serious breach of responsibility on the part of the counselor (and his agency) to the client he serves. Many times, these acts are, as the lawyers say, "actionable," i.e., you and your agency could be sued.

A drug treatment specialist smokes dope with her client. A therapist sleeps with his patient. A case manager steals a valuable piece of jewelry from an elderly client's home. A nurse steals drugs from the hospital and uses them herself while she is on duty. In other settings these might be called violations of the company's work rules or gross misconduct; in the arena of human services we call them serious ethical violations.

Exactly how a supervisor and agency should respond to a hanging offense is not for me to say, especially since there are always extenuating circumstances. However, I will submit to you that an agency (and especially one receiving tax dollars) will be held to a higher standard of conduct by its community than will a private practitioner who commits the same offense.

The private therapist who is publicly exposed for his sleeping with patients may suffer a loss of patients and income, a possible spanking from his professional association, a possible temporary loss of license, and, if found guilty as charged in a civil court action (provided such action is even taken), he and his insurance company may have to pay some damages. But an agency similarly exposed can be ruined.

Once the press or the rumor mill has got its teeth into something as juicy as a possible scandal in your agency, it doesn't really matter whether you were technically right or wrong or have had your day in court or have taken wise and considered action relative to the offender. What matters is how badly the innuendo stinks.

It may give you a bit of courage (when you are in the middle of a decision to fire or not to fire an employee who has committed what he or she *knows* to be a hanging offense) to remember that your clients include not only those already in your agency, but also all those yet to come to you from your community. Being accused by the press of wrist slapping, or taking half-measures, or protecting an errant staffer who has clearly crossed the lines of professional conduct can be, simply put, devastating to the purpose and mission of your organization. Funding sources, though I'm sure they would never admit it, might also shade their decisions in favor of an organization less sullied by "perceived" improprieties.

So, when you are confronted with a serious and intentional ethical violation or something everyone in our field would agree is the equivalent of a capital offense, schedule a big meeting with all the key players, (including the agency's attorney if you are going to act quickly or there are questions of law), and lay out your plan of action. Since emotions tend to run high in these sorts of meetings, try to have a least one cool head in the room—preferably someone with no vested interest in the outcome.

Other Problems

Short of hanging offenses, what are the other things staff do or don't do to warrant termination?

I break these down into productivity problems and attitude problems.

Productivity in mental health services generally translates to direct services; seeing X number of clients per week, getting reports done on time, meeting the paperwork requirements—all the sorts of things you have a right to expect and should be able to measure.

For reasons never clear to me, some people don't seem to feel obliged to put in a full day's work. Maybe they have a sense of entitlement that says to them, "This joint owes me a living." Maybe they think the pay is insufficient. Or maybe they don't really like patients. Frankly, after I've made all reasonable efforts to help them correct the productivity problem, I don't really care what reasons they might have for not doing the job the agency is paying them to do.

What I do care about is that such a person is not meeting expectations and, as a result, patients who need help are not getting it, taxpayer's money is being wasted and, very often, morale is suffering because this person is willing to let everyone else on the team carry the heavy end of the board.

Assuming you have a way to measure output (more on this in another chapter), I can think of no reason an unproductive employee should not be brought around to the same standards expected of everyone else. It takes some work to establish and monitor such standards, but then that is what managers get paid to do. As noted elsehere, utter fairness in your treatment of *all* staff is the key to gaining high respect, fostering good morale, and getting the job done well.

Attitude Problems

The attitude problem is much more difficult to measure and, therefore, to confront head-on. Still, it can be done.

The expression of a bad attitude may be impossible to define but, to me at least, I know one when I see or hear one. And so do other staff. Therefore, my approach is to start a private file in my desk and begin to jot down behavioral evidence of the problem—remarks made in staff meetings, observations by others of similar behavior on and off campus and, especially, any interactions with patients wherein the attitude problem (usually some resentment toward a supervisor, another staffer, or the agency in general), is passed along to the patient.

The moment patient care is endangered by a staff member with an attitude problem, e.g., "You're lucky you're seeing me . . . this whole place is run by idiots," I have no problem acting quickly and decisively. But more often than not, you don't get this kind of golden opportunity or irrefutable evidence of misconduct. More likely, you will have to collect such bits and pieces of information over a long period until, in the end, you've enough circumstantial evidence to take the person to the mat and insist on a change in the attitude, or that they move on.

As an aside, I might note that I've not had much luck in helping people change a bad attitude, especially if it is directed at the agency's leadership. Barring a change in this leadership, a staffer who has publicly complained for months about what a rotten outfit he has to work for and who has intentionally undermined the authority and effectiveness of the management team has, like the chap who conspired to overthrow the king, put his neck a bit too far into the noose—tighten it a little and most of these folks can be helped to move along.

I should also comment that sometimes the expression of a bad attitude down in the ranks is the result of covert approval of such an attitude by the employee's supervisor who, it often turns out, shares similar feelings about the organization but because of his administrative position, cannot express them publicly. Therefore, if you are presented with a continuing attitude problem in a particular department or program, it is well to remember that when you are setting your sights on who needs firing, you may be aiming too low.

Insubordination (the outright refusal to carry out a reasonable request for performance) is a subset of the attitude problem and, usually, makes a firing much simpler. However, be sure that you, or the supervisor who works for you, did not trigger the act of defiance. Since most acts of anger/insubordination have been set off by the action or inaction of someone else (the supervisor recommending the termination?), every effort must be made to carefully review *all the circumstances* leading up to the offense in question. Before executing a summary dismissal of an employee for an act of insubordination, at least two cool heads other than those "offended" need to quietly review the entire episode. In the heat of these circumstances, more time is your strongest ally.

There are many other reasons to let people go, but in the interest of brevity, I will now move to the steps you need to take to get this part of your job done.

1. Collect the needed data. These will include performance reports, absenteeism reports, notes from supervisory meetings during which these problems were discussed, a job deficiency report, and any and all observations pertinent to the action you are about to take.

2. Schedule a meeting with your boss (and personnel if you have someone in this capacity) and thoroughly review your recommendation to fire. Hopefully, someone in that meeting will take the role of the devil's advocate and challenge you on your decision. Provided you've lined up your ducks in a neat and convincing row, you should leave this meeting with a firm commitment to act. You should feel fully supported by the CEO *and* personnel. You should also know that you are on firm legal ground.

3. Decide who you want to be with you when you terminate the employee. Someone from personnel? Your director? Given

how awful these sessions can go, doing it all by yourself can sometimes be a mistake. I've done it both ways; don't like it much in any form.

However, if you expect trouble, have someone with you—if only as a witness.

4. Schedule the meeting. Short notice is best. Oftentimes the staffer knows she's in serious trouble and may be anticipating the worst when you ask for a separate meeting with her. Since there is no point in everyone's being agonized any longer than necessary, a few hours to a day should be long enough for anyone to wait.

Most people are fired on Fridays. According to my friends in personnel work, this is the worst possible day to let someone go, since he is left alone for a weekend during which he cannot seek other employment. Friday firings should be avoided. Monday or Tuesday are best since, with almost a full week to get busy seeking another job, at least the person is not further immobilized by the calendar and left to fume and stew over the weekend.

5. Whatever else you do once the interview starts, don't waver in your resolve. If you've never fired someone before, I recommend you do some role-playing with someone as preparation. Know what you want to say, how you will say it, and what you will say if the person questions the action.

Any signs or symptoms of uncertainty on your part may be interpreted by the employee as an indication that *you* are making a mistake by firing *them*. If you don't want to end up in a grievance procedure or courtroom defending your decision, carry out this action with all the calm, collected confidence you can possibly muster.

6. The good termination interview (and there are good ones) should not be a surprise to the employee. Upon getting the word, if they say something like, "I figured something like this was going to happen," you will have proof positive that you did your job well. Therefore, the interview should be short. Fifteen minutes should do it.

If a termination interview starts to drag on (longer, say, than thirty minutes) something is going wrong. Does the employee not believe you mean what you're saying? Are you giving hints there still might be some way they can redeem themselves? Are you trying to do crisis counseling?

My advice: Get it over with! Remember, part of the reason they pay you is to shoot the wounded.

7. If you want the person off the premises as soon as possible (as opposed to a more amicable termination where you've agreed to accept a resignation and the person will return to work to finish up loose ends), be sure you have the following in hand: his final paycheck (including payment for any vacation, overtime, travel expenses, etc.), a statement of any company benefits that will endure beyond his termination date (medical coverage, retirement funds, etc.), and all other details as are required when a person leaves the agency under the best of circumstances.

Note: when letting someone go for a bad attitude or gross insubordination or a clear violation of an important ethical standard, clearing them out fast is the best medicine. Rather than have staff and patients upset by a malcontent who has been let go but hangs around stirring up trouble, just have done with it—pay him off and move him out.

8. Be sure to communicate that the firing decision is both final and nonnegotiable. Since no one likes to be treated casually, you might say something like, "This was a difficult decision, but I want you to know that we have discussed this action at the highest levels of the agency and that everyone is in agreement that this is the right course."

To which the employee may ask, "Does the CEO know?"

Your answer should be a firm yes.

This is also the time to remind them of any grievance procedures available to them. However, if you've done your homework and are convincing in your words and actions, almost no one will attempt to challenge your decision—either informally or formally.

Some Final Observations

Try to avoid needless cruelty to someone you are firing. Having maintenance clean out his office and hand him a box of personal items can make a person feel like a thief. Encourage him to seek work elsewhere as soon as possible. If you can, offer to give a positive recommendation to his next employer. Unless you think he will steal the silverware, let him keep a key to the building so that he can clear his things out after closing hours. (But be sure to set a time and date certain to retrieve the key, or maintenance will kill you.)

If for any reason you treat people badly during a firing, you may set in motion an anger that can only be satisfied when the person contacts a lawyer and files a suit against you and your agency. Frivolous or not, such suits are often a needless by-product of a necessary severing of a relationship between your agency and the employee.

If you fire someone perfectly (following progressive discipline and with a serious but civil attitude) you may even be thanked for your action. That may sound odd, but I've seen it happen more than once.

Also, it may be helpful to think of a firing as having the following good results:

1. The person you just fired may undergo a vital change in self-awareness. He may suddenly realize that he needed to do something about himself, his attitude, his work habits and how he intended to be in this world. I've seen many fired people go on to better, more successful careers—not only in mental health, but in other fields as well.

2. You will often gain credibility, respect, and good power from both above (your boss) and below (your staff), for taking a right action at the right time.

3. You will, more or less immediately, begin to sleep better and be less crabby at home.

One last word. Firing a staffer who is well liked and loved by other staff and who, because you know of some misbehavior (usually an ethical violation) that requires you to terminate him summarily, can net you a lot of grief from your subordinates. They may interpret your action as sudden, unwarranted, unjustified, even cruel and unethical.

However, unless you are prepared to include all your staff in all your decisions about each of them (a level of participatory democracy practiced in no place on this planet of which I am aware), you are just going to have to buck up and take your lumps over the short term. Since word seems to eventually leak out about the "real reason" Harry was canned, the people who hate you today will eventually come around, and your stock with them, thank goodness, will quietly go back up.

Now, the next time you have to fire someone, don't forget to take yourself to dinner.

9

Let Ethics Be Your Guide

Not long ago I had occasion to work with a manager from the world of business. Among other things, he was troubled by his company's apparent insensitivity to the needs of its own employees. He complained of excessive workloads (including his own), self-serving personnel policies, disregard of stress-related problems among the employees, high turnover, and other signs and symptoms of what he described as a "slash and burn" company attitude. To add to his burden, he had recently learned of some possibly illegal practices by those above him—practices about which he was expected to remain silent. As you might guess, my client was experiencing a serious crisis of values and some associated symptoms of guilt and anxiety.

I asked, "What are your company's ethical standards?"

"I dug them out of our procedures manual the other day," he said. "Frankly, I was surprised to find we had any." Then he laughed. "They must have been written by an accountant."

"How so?"

"The first rule is, 'Employees will not steal from the company.' The second rule is, 'Employees who learn of other employees who are stealing from the company will report them immediately.'"

"That's it?"

"Just about," he said. "We're not supposed to bribe politicians or take kickbacks or sell company information, but it doesn't say anything about how we're supposed to treat our employees, our

110

customers, or the competition. Pretty self-serving if you ask me."

I didn't disagree with him.

In this chapter, I want to do two things: suggest a way in which to operationalize ethical principles so that the manager's job can be made easier and, secondly, at least touch on the subject of risk management and how to avoid lawsuits. The two subjects, ethical practice and risk management, go hand in hand, and always have.

Unlike the worlds of business and commerce and politics, we clinicians and counselors are positively burdened down with ethical standards. Most of us came from the professional cradle with a pretty clear set of notions about what is fair and right with respect to how we work with the people we serve. Originating in ancient medicine and the special responsibilities of the shaman, we are still fussing with them. And as our healing knowledge and technology increase, our burden to care for others increases and, with this obligation to "do no harm," our ethical sensitivities grow apace. Or should.

Each of the major helping professions has a detailed set of ethical standards, standing national ethics committees, as well as state and local ethics committees. State licensing agencies are increasingly incorporating professional ethical standards (and adherence thereto) into the requirement for licensure or certification in nursing, psychiatry, psychology, social work, marriage and family counseling, addictions specialists, and other service provider groups. In a word, our ethical standards are becoming law and, thereby, the standard of practice is rising, the consumer is enjoying better protection, and the lawyers are finding it easier to sue us.

Some agencies have oaths of confidentiality, others have standards of conduct that oblige staff to behave in proscribed ways. Every employer of a health service provider expects adherence to the ethical standards of the employee's particular profession. Directors of agencies are increasingly taking an interest in this business of ethical practice, and for one simple reason: The majority of successful lawsuits brought against mental health practitioners are the direct result of clear ethical violations. (More of this later.)

One of the problems with breaches of ethical practice in the field is that few graduate schools spend much time teaching ethics. Professors may cover ethics as part of a professional issues course and, certainly, pastoral counselors have had plenty of training in ethics but, except for explicit obligations of law (child abuse reporting requirements, etc.) formal ethical training for clinicians and counselors is pretty sparse. Even more interesting; professional ethics within the context of these changing times are a fluid, constantly evolving set of notions that, unless you keep up, can quickly get away from you.

But a comprehensive review of professional ethics is not what this chapter is about. What this chapter is about is how you, as a manager, can use a few critical ethical standards to make your life easier, your decisions clearer, and help keep your agency, staff, and clients out of troubles both little and big.

Having taught an ethical issues course to mental health providers for the past fifteen years, I will cut directly to the chase and give you what I think are the key ingredients to good decision making based on ethical principles. I have, by the way, borrowed these ideas from social work, psychology, nursing, psychiatry, and any other profession that had the wisdom to contribute to our professional sense of right and wrong.

Client Welfare

First, no decision is value free. Even deciding whether to use real butter on your toast (according to my friends who've had open heart surgery) is a value-laden decision. As managers of people helpers, I would argue that *all* our choices are heavily weighted by our values—which is why, when you must make dozens of them each day, it is essential to know around which core values you are shading your decisions.

For all of us, the core value is the same: client welfare. It is a simple value. It states that it is better to help people than to be negligent of or harmful to them. It is around this value that our professional lives turn. It is our guiding principle and is, unless I am mistaken, at the core of every professional ethical standard.

To hold to this principle, we are professionally obliged not only to preserve and protect the individual human rights of each client by way of adherence to law and statute, but to do a great deal more as well. Being civil toward, considerate of, and respectful to our clients, for example. In common behavioral terms, being on time for appointments, considering the client's point of view about the treatment she is about to receive, and being scrupulously honest with those who rely on us for help are just a few of the practices that define the behavior of the professional.

In my own view, it is not enough for managers in our professions to just follow the laws as they are written. There is more to it than that. Managers set the tone for how staff respond to client's needs and sensitivities. If you'll forgive the wording, managers carry the moral standards of the agency or institution. If you've a manager who cares only about his own ego and ambitions and thinks of client welfare last, then you will likely find this attitude reflected in his staff.

I could be wrong about this loading of additional moral and ethical responsibility on the shoulders of managers, but I remember very clearly an unpleasant incident in which, for reasons of a gross ethical violation, I had to fire someone who had worked for one of my supervisors for several years. As we neared the end of the termination interview, the man said, "I feel so bad about all of this. Especially for you, Paul. . . . I know how my actions violated your ethical standards."

My ethical standards!? I have often wondered how rapaciously this staff person might have behaved had he assumed (or known) my responsibilities to clients was no more enlightened than his.

As our values and attitudes are acquired via social learning and since you can't write enough procedures to direct the everyday use of common sense or ethical behavior, I believe we managers are stuck with this duty to bear, model, and teach the highest possible principles of professional conduct for our staffs. The obligation is, as I see it, unavoidable.

Putting Ethics to Work

While it is true that character and integrity have little need for written rules, it falls to us managers to tell our staffs when something is wrong. Sometimes we can do this in a kindly, educational fashion (the preferred method), but sometimes we must be perfectly blunt, and occasionally brutal. But that is okay. Working from an ethical stance gives you the power to use whatever power you need to get the job done.

To get everyone on staff on board about what is expected by way of ethical behavior, I think it is important that an agency have a document that defines the standards of conduct expected for all its employees. Called "work rules" in many settings, and "uniform codes" in the branches of the military, these standards vary from place to place, time to time, and according to the nature and mission of the organization. More importantly, while every manager has a right to expect each of her staff to abide by the highest professional standards of his particular profession she has, in addition, a right to expect adherence to other standards of conduct as well, including those deemed important by her own agency.

I might add that since many agencies and institutions are staffed by volunteers, cooks, maintenance people, receptionists, word processors, drivers, and others who have not necessarily had any exposure to ethical training or standards (and yet represent liability to the agency if they should breach, say, confidentiality), *everyone* working in the agency needs to be aware of the agency's policies with respect to client welfare and the obligations attached thereto.

While I am sure there are many such standards of conduct to consider, the following were adopted for all staff (clinical, support, student, and volunteers) at the Spokane Community Mental Health Center where I work. Skipping the preamble of obligation to maintain one's own particular professional standards and editing them for brevity, here are the essential parts:

1. Staff shall protect the welfare of the client by maintaining the highest standards of confidentiality as prescribed by law.

2. Staff shall accurately represent professional qualifications, associations, and affiliations.

3. Professional staff shall provide treatment services only in the context of a professional relationship and not by means of newspapers, magazine articles, radio or television programs, or other forms of mass media.

4. All staff shall refrain from dual relationships with clients

including, but not limited to, relationships of sexual intimacy. Dual relationships may include becoming personal friends, entering into a business transaction, or receiving valuable gifts, favors, or services from clients. It is understood that the therapist/client relationship exists beyond the client's formal termination.

5. Staff shall, in normal circumstances, only offer professional services to persons not concurrently receiving counseling assistance from another professional, except with knowledge of the other professional.

6. Ethical concerns about one's own actions or those of other staff should be discussed with your supervisor.

7. Staff shall be free from alcohol or other drug misuse for a period of two years immediately prior to the time of employment, and shall under no circumstances render services to clients while under the influence of alcohol or other drugs.

8. When staff members are aware of circumstances within the agency that are felt to impair the effectiveness, morale, and efficacy of delivery of services to clients, they shall make every effort to bring about positive change through appropriate channels. If, however, their views of the agency's response to their efforts to bring about change remain at odds with the agency, they shall refrain from behavior, either publicly or within the agency, which causes the agency public embarrassment or results in poor morale, lowered effectiveness, and damage to the therapeutic atmosphere of the agency and its clients.

9. Staff shall make every effort to avoid public situations that could be construed as improper and, since staff are always representing the agency (even when off duty), they should conduct themselves in a professional manner in all circumstances.

10. Staff shall make every effort to maintain positive relationships with clients, client's families, advocates, and all other agencies with whom we work.

As you can see, some of these standards are repetitive of standards in many of the mental health professions. They are in no way exhaustive. I will focus here on those standards that can be put to work to make the manager's job easier and, as these things tend to run together, will deal with risk management more specifically later on. The bottom-line managerial question is always the same: How will my decision best protect and forward client welfare?

Dual Relationships

The matter of dual relationships (item #4) is one that should concern every manager, since this is the area where staff tend to get into trouble. Problems of sexual intimacy are fairly straightforward and fall under the rubric of "hanging offenses" (see chapter on firing); however, it is the not-so-obvious other dual relationships with which we must often deal.

I cannot detail for you all the possible ways in which client welfare can be endangered by a staff member who, with or without conscious awareness, may traffic in the needs of his client to satisfy needs of his own. From motives as innocent as the need of a personal friendship to those as sinister as subjecting a client to one's own will for purposes of power or control or money, the smart manager will assume nothing, but suspect that *anything* is possible. So long as you remain aware that the client's welfare must come first, making these Solomon-like determinations and taking the necessary action to protect clients will be much easier.

Having many friends in rural mental health, I also know that total avoidance of dual relationships is essentially and, from a practical standpoint, impossible. A counselor has to buy groceries from an ex-client, counsel the sheriff's son, or may serve on the PTA with a current client. In such settings dual relationships are simply unavoidable. Even so, the manager's job still requires that clients never be advantaged by staff because of the special relationship that accrues between the client and the agency.

A fellow manager friend of mine has put this whole problem of potential abuse of clients via dual relationships into a simple prohibition: "If you can't chart it, don't do it!" I can think of no better way to put it.

Reporting Ethical Concerns

The obligation to ask about ethical concerns (item #6), is as near to pie in the sky as I will come in this book. Truly unethical people only "get ethical" when they're about to get caught. I haven't much hope that such a dictum will bring about any real change in someone whose basic character is unencumbered by the burden of scruples. (In my darker moods about the nature of man, I sometimes find myself siding with Mark Twain when he wrote, "An ethical man is a Christian holding four aces.")

But raising the sense of obligation for staff to come forward with ethical concerns about their own actions, or about the actions of others, can be helpful to the agency—especially if the manager's attitude is one of "let's talk about these things before something bad happens." If nothing else, we can at least hope that once staff are made aware of the ethical dimensions of their work, they may come to us for clarification or guidance. And while we may not always have the answer to some budding ethical problem, at least we will have had a chance to struggle with it. In my view, it is essential that staff at least know to whom they are supposed to take such problems (us).

Drug and Alcohol Abuse
The business of misusing or abusing alcohol and/or drugs while on or off duty (item #7) is a complex one and I won't try to examine all the possible risks to which a client might be put when his therapist is abusing, addicted, or otherwise in trouble with chemicals. It is enough to say that a standard of conduct on drug and alcohol abuse has entered the people-helping field from the professions of drug and alcohol counselors and, in my opinion, not a minute too soon.

Whatever your agency's feelings or policies about drug and alcohol use by its staff, it is my opinion that some sort of statement needs to be made about the agency's position—both at the time of hiring, and as it applies to current members of the staff. With all the hullabaloo about drug abuse in our culture just now, it ought to be clear to employees of every kind just what his or her employer's attitudes are on the subject.

Having directed a drug treatment program for many years, it is a matter of common sense (as well as law in my state) that we do not hire someone currently in trouble with drugs or alcohol. Appropriately credentialed people with two years of sobriety prior to the day of hiring is our minimum standard.

Question: Since all kinds of clients outside of formal chemical dependency treatment programs have primary or secondary problems with alcohol, street drugs, or prescription drugs, should *all* professional people helpers be held to the same standard of no misuse?

I think they should, but that's only because it's my personal view that a great many professionals routinely underdiagnose substance abuse. Inadvertently, they enable their clients to continue to use chemicals that not only put them at risk of serious accident injuries to themselves and others, but also aid and abet their continuing dependence on, and addiction to, mind-altering and destructive drugs. In a word, too many of us waste precious clinical hours treating the wrong problem.

But be that as it may, a manager must sometimes make decisions about staff based on such tenuous data as secondhand reports of substance abuse. To hear that a staff person had four martinis for lunch and then returned to the office to counsel his clients may not be a problem you can reach and stop on a first report. But if you've an articulated standard about the unacceptability of such conduct, then you can act. The bottom-line question is, again, client welfare: Would you want your best friend counseled by someone who just polished off four martinis?

I don't have ready answers to questions about the effect of killer hangovers or casual marijuana use (if there is any), or of so-called recreational use of cocaine on the welfare of clients. This sort of research isn't done and, considering who would need to be the subjects in such an experiement, isn't likely to be done.

But what I do know is that what may be acceptable drug use for lawyers or loggers or Laundromat managers, is not necessarily acceptable drug use for professional people helpers. And when you consider the statutory intolerance and severe consequences of drug or alcohol abuse for commercial airline pilots, nuclear plant workers, policemen and women, and any of those our society has sanctioned as responsible for our physical welfare it seems, to me at least, that people-helping professionals ought not to be held to a lesser standard. It is something we might all think about.

Staff Views of the Agency
This is a tough one (item #8) and comes to us from the social work standard that says, in effect, that one should not continue

to work for an evil empire once you know it is evil and have made every good effort possible to try to change it. An ethical social worker, aware of his agency's malfeasance or misdirection, either works to change the agency so that it operates morally on behalf of its clients, or he quits.

What you don't do if you're dissatisfied with your agency is sit around and grouse about what a lousy, rotten outfit you work for and, thereby, wreck the morale of your fellow workers and endanger the welfare of the clients who are trying to get help.

I like this standard not only because it addresses the system's problems (there are evil empires), but because it gives the manager a very good and powerful tool with which to deal with a staff person whose negative attitude toward the agency seems unadjustable through the application of usual and customary supervisory methods.

I don't mind staff grousing or complaining about things and, in fact, get a little nervous if there isn't a certain background level of bitching going on. But what I do mind is that staff person whose constant negative attitude undermines the morale and, therefore, the therapeutic effectiveness of the rest of the staff which, in both the short and the long term, endangers client welfare. (I have covered this subject in the chapter on firing as well, but since it is so dear to me, I'll indulge myself a bit and be redundant.)

Assuming that, in fact, you and your staff are not working for some evil empire, then after you have exhausted all the reasonable approaches to bring about the changes a disgruntled staff person feels are needed, then I think you have a right to ask that staff person to do the ethical thing: shut up or resign.

This may sound a bit harsh and like a high-stakes move, but I think you will find that the quality of life for you, your staff and your clients will dramatically improve once you have adopted and adhere to this particular standard. Just be certain, of course, that in your own mind you are working for a benevolent agency with benevolent leadership.

Public Appearance of Propriety
Elsewhere in this book I have alluded to the fact that people helpers and people-helping agencies and institutions are held to a higher standard of conduct than the private practitioner in

solo or even group practice. Therefore, the adoption of a standard of public conduct (item #9), while difficult if not impossible to enforce, at least sets the tone for how staff should behave even while off campus.

Again, the sole purpose for such a standard relates ultimately to the welfare of the clients—those currently receiving services and those who may, one day, wish to seek your services.

I won't bore you with stories that have floated around my own community after one staff member or other engaged in some disreputable public activity, but I will tell you that I have seen entire agencies badly damaged by the arrest and conviction of one of its staff members.

But of even more concern is that, since we *are* our reputations in this business, the lonely, frightened, needy, and sometimes overly cautious client (who is suspect of psychologists and our ilk in the first place) certainly doesn't need to see one of our esteemed staff falling down drunk in a public restaurant the night before her first appointment. Neither will she be comforted by observing a staff member walking into an hourly rate motel room with someone she knows to be a client of the agency.

There is a Vietnamese saying that covers this potential for public misinterpretation of one's behavior rather well, and while I will apologize for accuracy of the translation, it goes roughly as follows: "Do not comb your hair while walking through your neighbor's orchard." In sum, why borrow trouble?

Maintaining Positive Relationships

This standard (item #10) was contributed by the executive director of a mental health center (one of the people to whom this book is dedicated) who, after a lifetime of community-based work, is acutely aware of the need for fostering cordial and positive working relationships between all the agencies, families, advocates, and other people involved in the complicated networks of systems and services, which, working together, try to reduce human suffering.

For the clinical or counseling professional who only sees clients, this may be a difficult standard to understand or accept.

But to the manager it is one that can be very valuable when it comes to getting the superordinate goals of the agency accomplished, i.e., seeing as many people as effectively and efficiently as possible with limited resources, avoiding bureaucratic hassles and delays, etc. It might better be called an ethical standard for any community social service agency.

At least a few clinicians and counselors see no particular need to get along with other agencies, a client's family members, a client's advocate or lawyer or friend, or anyone who is not a specific part of the specific problem their client has come to them to solve. This is not only too bad, it is shortsighted.

How many problems are created as a direct result of a counselor who takes the position that nobody counts in the helping relationship except him and his client, no one will ever know. But this "center of the universe" attitude is probably responsible for more hard feelings, miscoordination, and ultimate risk and damage to the welfare of clients than any other perspective of which I can think. Social workers know this well, I wish the rest of us did.

With this standard of conduct in place—that staff will make every effort to maintain positive relationships with others in the client's life—at least you have opened the door for staff to learn about why it is important not to intentionally (or even unintentionally) offend others in the system. This does not mean that others in the system may not need offending, it only means that your agency's foreign policy needs to be diplomatic to a fault, aimed at community integration (not disintegration), and that all staff should extend the open hand of friendship first, not, as I have too often heard, "over my dead body."

If you've been a manager for a while then you know how clients can sometimes get caught between two warring agencies and, as a result, suffer from a systems problem that seems to be staffed by the social service equivalent of the Hatfields and McCoys. I think all of us, and especially our clients, could benefit from a bit more mutual acceptance of each other's reality and a bit less ethnocentrism.

Risk Management and Malpractice

While I cannot hope to address the whole area of malpractice and risk management in our field, let me just say that if a clinical decision is ethically sound and professionally sound, it will be legally defensible.

As of this writing, the malpractice crisis is spreading into the mental health field and, with the attendant high premiums for insurance coverage, community impact of lawsuits against helping agencies, and the general bad press we all get when clients go public with claims of damages, managers need to take special care and caution to avert, as the lawyers say, "potentially compensable events." As was suggested earlier, good ethical practice means fewer successful lawsuits.

It may be worth remembering that with the increasing autonomy of practitioners and the increasing authority given mental health professionals and their agencies from the courts and legislatures, our rising profile as care givers also gives plaintiffs' lawyers a better target. My lawyer friends, who used to specialize in suing only MDs, are now spreading their glad tidings to PhD's, MAs, social workers, nurses, and just about anyone who would presume to earn a living by assuming some responsibility for the mental health of others.

Here, briefly, are the major areas where suits are filed and where, since you are a risk manager, you might wish to focus your worry time:

- Medication-related cases. Restricted to physicians and nurses, suits here are based on negligence, e.g., failure to properly prescribe or failure to properly monitor medication effect.
- Seduction allegation. The result of a dual relationship and a failure to deal with the transference, these suits are based on the patient's having received substandard care. Emotional distress damages are increasingly easy to prove as lawyers become more familiar with the case law in this area and, as a result, the cases are proliferating.
- Failure to warn. Although state laws vary here, it is clear most courts hold mental health professionals and/or their parent agencies to the so-called duty-to-warn standard.
- Failure to protect the patient from himself. Wrongful death suits based on negligence, these are almost always successful suicides that the court or jury was convinced could have been prevented.

- Although only being talked about and developed now, I expect considerable confusion, court action, and possibly the greatest ethical debate and dilemma in modern times to emerge around the subject of how to care for the mental health and physical needs of those suffering from acquired immunodeficiency syndrome (AIDS).

The Manager's Job

As a manager you are already responsible for reducing risks in your agency or hospital. It's another one of those jobs they left out of your job description. But how, you may ask, do you do this?

A sometimes cynical social worker pal of mine says, "all the ethics in the world won't change human nature." I hope he's wrong, but even if he isn't, ethical standards, all by themselves, are not enough to reduce your risk of a malpractice action. No, you need to do some specific things.

Here, and even though this is only a brief review, are a few of the things that give structure and strength to the fine ideals of ethical principles. These will, by the way, hold you in good stead if you should end up in court:

- Documentation. The patient's chart is not only a record of the services he received, it is his protection against abuse or negligence. It is also the most important protection an agency has against allegations of wrongful conduct. Whether an action may later on be viewed as wrong makes no difference. Chart everything.
- Incident reports. However you define an incident, the written report of what happens should lead to an analysis of the problem and possible procedural changes so that there will be no recurrence of the same problem in the future. If you think something you did or failed to do would look stupid or negligent to a layman, as in, "Gee, Ed, seems to me that was a pretty dumb thing to do," then it probably was an incident and should be handled as such.
- Quality-assurance committees. Too complicated to go into here, part of the Q-A committee's job should be to do the thinking work on the incident reports and come up with long-term solutions to acute, risk-to-patient situations.

- Patient advocates. Not every system has a patient-advocate system or consumer representation on governing or advisory boards, but when it comes to keeping ethical practice and even-handed, civil behavior a constant in a care system, advocates can have a salutary and important role.
- Multidiciplinary communication. When everyone is clearly talking to everyone else (as evidenced by staff meetings where all the key players show up, sharing of clinical records, consistent patterns of information flow, up-to-date medical records, etc.) the chances for a major screwup and lawsuit are greatly reduced. In my experience, it's when people go off on their own (usually to do their own thing) that bad things happen (read: potentially compensable events).
- Physician input in questions of safety. Anytime the physical safety of patients is involved, MDs should be also. It's simple; courts, families, and juries consider the judgment of trained physicians the best available.
- Patient-satisfaction surveys. Not something you need to do all the time with every patient, such surveys give consumers a chance to complain. The fact that you do them can help keep everyone on the up-and-up and, from time to time, you may learn something very important.

As there are entire workshops devoted to the subject of how to avoid malpractice (and although I've stood accused, I am also *not* a lawyer), I won't extend this list or pretend to cover all that could be said on the subject. However, because it is the manager's job to reduce risks to clients, agency, and staff, I will suggest that such training could be very valuable.

I might only add here that in my experience there are three things that make people angry enough to sue; being treated in a high-handed fashion, being treated in a high-handed fashion, and being treated in a high-handed fashion. On the other hand, if you accept the possibility you or one of your staff may have made a mistake, always treat everyone with dignity and respect, you will likely head off a great many potential lawsuits.

Ethics or standards of conduct provide guidelines, but they don't change behavior. Therefore, it is only through careful hiring practices, thoughtful monitoring, good supervision, solid training, awareness of changing standards of care, and quick action when things go wrong, that the manager can hope to reduce risks to his clients and his agency.

I did not think this chapter would be so long. But I hope it has been worth the reading. My central point is that you, as a manager, have a right to expect ethical behavior and that staff abide by certain standards of conduct, whether they be their own professional standards or those written by the agency.

More, staff have a right to expect ethical behavior from you. When you bend an ethical rule for one staff person, you don't just bend it; you create a new rule. Do this more than once and if word gets out (and it always does), and you will be finished as an effective leader.

Clear standards, good procedures, and tight adherence to these can not only reduce your agency's risk of a lawsuit, but will set the tone for the entire agency's work and effectiveness. There is a certain power attainable through the practice of ethical standards, power that is not simply blind righteousness, but a kind of clear vision based on thought-out principles that, at least in my experience, gets done what we all want: the best possible service to people of which we are capable.

10

Time Management

$\mathbf{A}$s you are reading these words at this very moment and if you are seated at your desk at the office, I will make what should be a correct assumption; reading this book is the most important thing you can possibly be doing at this particular instant.

If I am wrong (that you have more important things to do right now) then maybe you should put this book down and get cracking on what needs doing first—which is, by the way, the first lesson in time management: Do what needs doing now, *now*.

But if you've got a couple of spare minutes, this is probably as good a place to invest them as any, especially since I hope by the time you've read this chapter you will have opened up at least several more hours a month in your schedule.

Thinking about Time

I don't know how it is for other people, but I have never been very good at procrastination or wasting time. The thought of "killing" time only reminds me that, in all its clever ways, time is killing me. So whether working or playing, I try never to piddle away that of which they only give you so much. For example, I've given myself one morning to write this chapter.

People managers, if nothing else, manage time: their own, as well as that of their staff. Given that it is available time for clients that is the major product of our agencies, I can think of nothing more important than the wise expenditure of it.

126

To clear up a couple of things that sometimes get confused, please ask yourself this question: What is it they pay me for?

If your answer is to be on the job forty hours a week, then you are still thinking about time and work very much like the guys I used to work with when I was a laborer in a steel mill. Yes, we were supposed to get some work done, but the most important thing was that our time cards showed forty hours. If you didn't put in forty hours of time (warm body, physically present), they didn't give you forty hours of pay.

Thinking this way about time and work is an old habit for most of us, but one we must break if we're to think like managers.

If your answer as to why they pay you is that you are a problem solver, that you work smarter not harder, and that you make good decisions (versus produce buckets of sweat), then maybe it will make sense to you that the forty hours you spend each week on the job are, in actuality, an artifact of the industrial revolution, primarily required of you by way of setting a good example for others, and so that you will be available to your staff when they need you.

The fact is, you should not have to be on the job anything like forty hours a week to do it well. Sometimes thirty hours will be plenty. Sometimes thirty-five. On average, it will take forty. But it frequently will take fifty and sometimes sixty hours to do it right. To think like a manager you need a rubber watch—one that stretches time any which way it has to; just so long as there is enough of it to get the important things done.

From my causal reading of the *Wall Street Journal* each morning, I have repeatedly read that most managers in business and industry spend more (not less) than forty hours a week working for their companies. It isn't written into their job descriptions, but more than forty hours is the norm and, generally, expected. Many chief executive officers routinely spend in excess of fifty hours a week. Most, it seems, are happy to put in this kind of time and wouldn't be satisfied with themselves if they didn't. For most managers, it is the quality of the job they do and how they feel about their work that matters, not the time it takes to do it.

In my own experience, the manager's job never really ends.

If some big problem needs attention, a manager tends to work on it until it is solved—after the close of regular business hours, on the weekends, and, sometimes, in the middle of the night when we are supposed to be having pleasant dreams. If our agencies paid us overtime for all the worry time, think time, fret time, and puzzling-at time we spend on problems off the premises and beyond the forty-hour standard work week, we could probably bankrupt our organizations.

So, to make life a little easier, throw away any old notions you once had about the so-called forty-hour work week. You don't have to produce buckets of sweat or a given number of widgets to be a good manager, but you do have to be smart and you do have to get the job done . . . no matter how long it takes.

Sometimes just sitting at your desk with your feet up or staring out the window at a passing cloud while you think about how to solve some problem or other is the most important thing you possibly do, and doing so should not cause you one minute's guilt. (I do, however, recommend you close your office door while engaged in this sort of high-level executive function.)

Priority Setting

Doing the most important thing first has become the hallmark of good time management. How could anyone quarrel with such a notion? The trick is to decide which of the many tasks before you is the most important. And since I don't know your job, I can't answer that question for you. But I know someone who can.

Other things being equal and assuming your boss knows her business and what it is she wants from you, a direct supervisor is always the best source of guidance about how to spend your time as a manager. There should be no embarrassment to asking the question: Which of these important things is most important? In fact, lack of clarity in expectations on this issue is probably one of the chief reasons managers fail to satisfy their supervisors.

Once you know what to do first, second, third, and so forth, your day automatically takes on some structure. Without some sort of structure into which to pour your energies, time seems to have a way of leaking out and slipping away. It is a very uncomfortable feeling for most of us to arrive at the end of the day and have the feeling that, somehow, we managed to fritter away eight or nine hours without accomplishing one bloody thing. Yet I often hear managers make this complaint. Structure helps avoid this feeling of time wasted.

My father has always been a very efficient manager of time and, as a teenager working in his business, he taught me a very valuable lesson about how to tackle huge piles of paperwork (forms, correspondence, memos, etc.).

"First," he said, "you stack your paperwork into three piles on your desk. This is the 'must' pile, and that means it must get done today. This second pile is the 'maybe' pile; if you get the 'must' pile done and there is still time, then you work on the 'maybe' pile. This third pile is the 'maybe not' pile. Once you have finished the 'must' pile and have worked all the way through the 'maybe' pile, only then may you start to work on the 'maybe not' pile."

"How do you know what papers to put in what piles?" I asked.

Dad smiled and tapped the side of his head. "That's why they give you brains."

Then I asked him, "What happens if you never get time to get to the 'maybe not' pile?"

"Oh," he said, "that's easy. At the end of the week, you just shove the 'maybe not' pile off into the wastebasket. You'll be amazed at how many 'maybe not' problems take care of themselves.

Check-off Lists and the Eighty/Twenty Rule

I know a few managers who, when you ask them to remember to do something, wink, write nothing down, and say, "Don't worry, I'll take care of it." These people make me nervous.

All the really efficient managers I know keep lists of things they need to get done. Frankly, as busy and complicated and memory testing as our work is, I don't see how people get along without check-off lists. I know I can't. I call mine the "Do" list. Each morning when I get to the office, I run down the "Do" list, pick off the most important phone call to return or memo that needs writing, or whatever, and start through what would be my father's "must" pile.

A "Do" list helps us follow the eighty/twenty rule. The eighty/twenty rule (first articulated by the Italian economist Vilfredo Pareto, who observed that of all the people in Italy, 20 percent owned 80 percent of the wealth) says that if you order all things on a list from most important to least important, 20 percent of what you do will yield 80 percent of the valuable results. Essentially, you learn to target the most important things first, do them, and let the rest go.

Here are some rough-and-ready predictions based on the eighty/twenty rule:

- 80 percent of sick leave will be taken by 20 percent of the staff
- 80 percent of the charting errors will be made by 20 percent of the staff
- 80 percent of the risk for a malpractice suit will come from 20 percent of the staff
- 80 percent of billing errors will be made by 20 percent of the clerks
- 80 percent of the no-shows will come from 20 percent of the clients

. . . and so forth. The point being, if you focus your efforts on those 20 percent of the problems that are giving you 80 percent of the headaches, you will be working smarter, not harder, and you will be getting a much bigger payoff for your time.

Some friends of mine use these time management, carry-around books that can help you organize your life twenty-four hours a day for the next couple of years. They swear by them. I can still get by with a pocket week-at-a-glance calendar, a checklist, and three piles of paperwork on my desk. I'd get even more organized, but once in a while I like to be overcome by an irresistible impulse, like sneaking out early to go fishing or to catch a movie.

Still, if you arrange your desk so that you have parking places for your paperwork, stop interrupting yourself by wasting time sorting through stacks of disheveled documents (get a tight filing system), work from a checklist and follow the eighty/twenty rule, you should at least *feel* like a more organized person.

Procrastination

I have a relative who is a great procrastinator. I get my birthday card never less than one month late every year and our Christmas gift generally arrives in February. He says he's going to do something about his procrastination, but he keeps putting it off.

Unless a piece of work is already in the "maybe not" pile, a manager cannot afford to keep putting off something that needs doing. Simply put, thinking about a problem and doing nothing about it is a waste of time. Not only is it a waste of time, but I think it is stress inducing to fuss at something and not move forward. Unresolved problems, high-priority work that is waiting to be done, reports that are overdue—all of these things make a manager's food go down in lumps. Why induce your own stress?

If the problem you are fussing at is a piece of paper (a letter you need to respond to, a grant that needs some editing, etc.), here's a simple test to see if you're wasting time.

Each time you pick up a piece of paper from your desk to study it or read it or reread it, try to take the necessary action before you put it down again. If you do set it down again, put a little pencil dot in the upper right-hand corner. The next time you pick it up to study it and do not act again, put another dot in the corner next to the first one.

Do this for one week with all the paper on your desk. At the end of the week, spread out all the paper and start counting dots.

Three dots in the corner of a piece of paper and you're pushing it; four, five, or more dots, and there is something wrong with that task. Since uncertainty is the most common item that clogs the drain, either you don't have the information you need to act (in which case you'd best go get it), or you need some other kind of input or help.

If you're racking up lots of dots on *all* the paperwork lying about your desk, then you've got a problem with priorities. As my friends in Alcoholics Anonymous say, "first things first."

Think about the four *D*'s of action: Do it, Delegate it, Delay it, or Dump it. If you don't want my father's "maybe not" pile sitting on your desk, open a delay drawer so that, rather than have a task low on the eighty/twenty list lying about staring at you and demanding attention, toss it in a drawer. Then, every so often, dump the drawer.

Whatever you must do to get the work of the week done, consider (for your own mental health) allowing yourself a little window of time toward the end of the week to finish up loose ends. I try to keep Friday's essentially open so that, even if it's been one of those miserable weeks when everything but the dog died, I can still polish off one or two little projects so that, as I head into the weekend, I can go out the door with a sense of having earned at least part of my salary.

The other *D* (delegation) is such a major time-saver that I have devoted an entire chapter to the subject.

All about Meetings

As I see it, there are three kinds of meetings: weekly staff meetings, clinical staff meetings, and problem-solving meetings. I'll describe how I think all three ought to work.

The Weekly Staff Meeting The purpose of the weekly staff meeting is to share information, discuss administrative changes or requirements, new procedures, what new clinical programs are available, and, generally, to keep the team informed about what's happening within the agency as well what is happening outside the agency that might affect their work. It's also the meeting in which, if you like, to dish a little dirt or pass on a funny story.

This meeting should take place at the same time and same place each week. Pick a time and place and stick to it. Humans are at least as habit-bound as milk cows, so if you change the time and place of this meeting willy-nilly, you will find about half the staff wandering out around in the pasture somewhere instead of in the meeting.

Start the meeting on time, and no later than five minutes

after the time you selected to begin. Let the latecomers catch up, but don't fritter away everyone's time.

Have an agenda. It can be simple, short, and added to at the meeting, but it is from agendas that structure is brought to any meeting. If you're the manager (and unless you've delegated this responsibility), you're responsible for the agenda.

End on time or sooner. People helpers have places to go and people to see; therefore, never let the meeting drag on past the maximum time allowed for it. If necessary, shelve whatever issue seems to be dragging on and come back to it the next week.

I say end a meeting "sooner" because, as often as not, a weekly staff meeting scheduled for an hour often doesn't need to take an hour. While it is true that work expands to fill the allotted time, there is no sense in sitting around filling the air with anecdotes if there are more important things to do. My staff meeting rule is this: Stop the meeting as soon as the work is done. Lots of my one-hour weekly staff meetings take thirty-five minutes, or less.

Attendance at the weekly staff meeting is desirable, but not essential. Since this is an information-sharing meeting, it is not critical that everyone be there—although that is always preferred. But if someone has a more important meeting, then the weekly staff meeting is one they can skip. (This is not true of the problem solving meeting I will get to in a minute.)

As the weekly staff meeting is a regularly scheduled meeting and should be on everyone's calendar, no notice needs to be sent.

You may or may not wish to write up a one-page summary of the meeting and what was discussed or shared. Such a summary is very helpful to those who could not attend, but there is also an expense associated with such paperwork. If the meeting is a big one (with more than ten people usually attending), then a mailed summary might be very useful. If in doubt, ask the group what they would like.

The Clinical Staff Meeting   The purpose of clinical staff meetings is, generally, to present new cases, staff old ones, and to help the treatment staff solve clinical problems. Like the weekly staff meeting, this meeting should always take place at the same time and place. No notice needs to be sent.

Some agencies have an "intake" staffing wherein all new cases are formally presented, usually to a multidisciplinary staff of professionals. If these meetings result in good treatment plans, they are good meetings; if they result in endless speculation about how many diagnoses can dance on the end of a case history, they are a waste of precious time. Whoever runs the intake staff meeting (and unless it is a Grand Rounds sort of training meeting specific to solving some diagnostic puzzle) should be responsible to see to it that the patient somehow benefits from all those high-powered people in attendance.

My only timesaving tip on intake staffings is that, after years of presenting cases in such meetings and after more years of running such meetings, a reasonably articulate and well-prepared counselor should take no more than seven to ten minutes to present a new case. But that's only if you establish that as your expectation . . . , otherwise it will take him or her up to fifteen or twenty minutes, maybe more. The subsequent clinical discussion, of course, may take much longer.

If no one's in a hurry, it's nice to be able to take the extra time to be completely thorough with every case. But more and more these days, this is becoming a luxury and staff need to be reinforced for being concise, accurate, and brief. (I've always hoped that when they come around to staffing my case, someone will say, "Gee, let's give this guy some extra time. . . . After all, he was a psychologist and one of us.")

As with any meeting, start on time and end on time. No record of what happened needs to be kept, except as required by regulation. I might add that when staffing ongoing cases, it is always a good idea to note in the client's chart that their case was formally staffed, what was discussed, and recommended. You never know when such documentation may come in handy.

Except for limiting the length of presentations or discussions, I have not been able to think of any clever ways to save time in clinical staff meetings. And since these meetings are at the heart of what happens to and for our clients, I'm not sure this is the place to try to save time.

The Problem-Solving Meeting The purpose of a problem-solving meeting is to try to avoid some mess or, if it is too late for that, then to clean up some mess. If you are a super manager you should never have to have a problem-solving meeting. I have one of these meetings a couple of times a year just to stay in shape.

The problem-solving meeting is task oriented and only scheduled when you have some specific job to do. You schedule such a meeting to *solve* something, not just talk about it. It is a special meeting and, hopefully, a one-time-only meeting.

If you're the manager responsible for the meeting, here are your tasks:

- Get all the key players to the meeting. Phone first, follow up with a reminder call or memo if the problem is critical (and you probably shouldn't have the meeting if it isn't). If you have anyone on the list of attendees who is unreliable at showing up at meetings, bug him to be there. These meetings are very costly, so everybody who needs to be there, *needs to be there.*
- Send an agenda (if there is one) with the reminder memo. If in doubt about who should be there, always err on the side of including too many people. If someone says he doesn't think he needs to be there, fine, at least you asked. It's when you forget to ask that people's noses get bent out of shape.
- Get whatever background information (memos, reports, shared written observations, etc.) to the people attending the meeting well in advance of the meeting. You don't need uninformed people at such a meeting and you sure don't want them reading while everyone else is working.
- Depending on the complexity of the problem and since mental health types love to talk, give yourself plenty of time to work through the problem. If you can schedule such a meeting at eleven in the morning, and it looks like it is going to last longer than an hour, you can order lunch in and keep working. Generally speaking, don't set this sort of meeting up late in the day—people are tired and some of

them would rather go home than see the task accomplished.

- Attendance at a problemsolving meeting is critical. In fact, if even one really key player is not there, it is better to just cancel the meeting rather than to waste time working on a solution that may be unacceptable to the absent person.
- After the meeting, write up what happened, what was decided, and send the summary to everyone who was originally invited. This summary should be as long as it takes to communicate how the mess was cleaned up or avoided and how similar problems will be handled in the future.

Some problem-solving meetings might take two hours, some three, some four, or even a whole day. But so long as they remain task oriented, they should have some end point. If they don't, then something is wrong.

What I so often hear (and what is so wasteful of time) is that some problem or other brings staff together to seek solutions and, failing to find one right away, another meeting is scheduled. Then another. Then another. Pretty soon you have a standing weekly meeting during which (heaven forbid) staff are working on "working through" their role definitions and "processing" some issue or other. Any time I hear about such ongoing meetings where people are defocused to the point of discussing their "roles," I figure they either need a stronger leader, have started a sub-rosa therapy group, or haven't enough to do.

The Committee Meeting   I haven't much to say about the committee meeting, except that in my view committees should only meet when there is some specific work that needs going. To meet once a week or once a month just so that everyone can stay in touch is no justification for anything except a social club. A standing committee is, in my view, little more than a problem-solving meeting with a fancy title.

A couple of final timesaving notes on meetings. About once every three months or so, take a few minutes to study your meeting obligations; you may find one or two you can stop attending or get someone else to attend.

And here is a potential big time-saver. Examine which weekly meetings can be changed to twice a month, or even once a month. I have been able to save several hours each month by reducing routine meetings to a minimum, especially with staff who know their jobs and don't need me butting into their work. In fact, I've had several managers who needed no scheduled meeting with me at all and could get along very well by calling me only when they needed help.

To underscore the importance of cutting meetings short when they don't need to go long (remember that 80 percent of the valuable work in a meeting is probably accomplished in 20 percent of the time), run this through your cost-benefit calculator:

Seven people are to attend a meeting. One is missing at the time the meeting starts. The other six wait ten minutes.

Six people × ten minutes = sixty minutes. Waiting ten minutes has wasted one staff hour or, in client equivalencies, one therapy hour has been lost, together with the billing for that hour.

Or consider a two-hour meeting that could have ended in one-and-a-half hours.

Six people × thirty minutes = one hundred and eighty minutes, or three hours of lost staff time. If these are high-priced staff (say worth fifty or sixty dollars an hour) then you've lost around a hundred and fifty dollars—minus, of course, the fees they might have generated seeing clients.

One final note on meetings; don't hold a five-hundred-dollar meeting to solve a fifty-cent problem. Ask yourself: Do I really need this meeting? Or can I set up a conference call? Can I send the material around and ask for comments? Can I handle this with what I like to call a "hallway consultation," as in, "Say, Phyllis, have you got a second, I need to check something out with you?"

Minimizing Interruptions

Interruptions are the curse of effective time management. Here are a few suggestions to get control of your life:

- Keep your office door closed unless you want drop-in traffic. Or at least position your desk so that it is not facing an open door. You're not being rude, just smart. But if you're working on the "maybe" or "maybe not" pile, you can leave the door open—that way staff will know you're available for consultation or even casual conversation. The worst combination is the manager who, desiring to have a so-called open-door policy, sits with his head buried in paperwork and never looks up when someone passes his office door except, of course, to scowl. Do me a favor, if you don't want to be interrupted, keep your door shut.
- Get control of your phone. However you do this, it only matters that you get control. Next to the single-tone radio alert that warns us we are under a nuclear attack, a ringing phone is the most demanding and damnable creation of the twentieth century. Like any one else, I have my own love-hate relationship with phones—my best advice is to let it know who's boss.

Some managers feel it is essential to take every call as it comes in. I try to, but never at the expense of someone sitting in my office with me (client or staff). The phone systems available these days are nothing short of modern miracles, so take whatever time it takes to study how to use yours effectively and so that you haven't set yourself up for needless interruptions. If you think you are not as conditioned as one of Pavlov's rats to the sound of a bell, try letting the damned thing ring.

- Can't get all your heavy thinking or the most time-consuming work done during the day because of all the crises and brushfires and bells going off? Then try going to the office at six or seven A.M. for a couple of days. There is nothing quite like the solitude of an empty agency at seven in the morning to triple your output. Many effective managers routinely work these hours two or three days a week and swear by them.

Learn to Dictate

If you don't now dictate your letters, reports, clinical summaries, or any other communications that run longer than a progress note, I strongly recommend you learn this skill. The time savings are simply wonderful. A report that takes one hour to write out by hand should take, with experience, no more than ten to fifteen minutes to dictate, and sometimes a lot less.

Having taught clinicians and counselors how to dictate for many years, I can safely report the following:

- Even PhD's can learn to do it.
- Your written/typed product will be much improved in both quality and appearance.
- You will save literally hundreds of hours each year.

As to tips to learning how to do it, here's what I teach:

- Begin with a hand-held machine with a thumb-operated control button. You have to be in charge from the get-go.
- Write out your report or letter in longhand and then *read* it verbatim into the machine.
- Write your next report with no conjunctions, more and more abbreviations, and skip the punctuation.
- Write even less into your subsequent manuscripts and begin relying primarily on an outline . . . central ideas, findings, lab reports, etc.
- Fading out more and more of the written word, now go to just headings or an outline.
- Finally, once you've built some confidence, spend some time with your word-processing people. Take their advice and guidance about how to dictate to heart—after all, they have to listen to you all the time.

If, for example, you have ten staff and each hand writes one report a week, your departmental time savings could be as high as eight hours a week (eight more clients seen?).

In summary, if you stop right now and examine your schedule for those meetings you can stretch out to every two weeks, those meetings you can stop attending all together, those meetings you can shorten by half with no loss of content or output, and then sort your paperwork into my father's three piles (shoving the "maybe not" pile into the round file right now), begin to follow the eighty/twenty rule, learn to dictate, stop handling paper more than once, and close your door while you bully your telephone into submission, you should find you have four or five or even six hours left over this month. Maybe more.

Now, being so wise and time efficient, I suggest you take yourself out to a leisurely dinner, shop that sale you saw in the paper, catch a movie, hit a bucket of golf balls, or otherwise enjoy some of those precious hours we all say we're working so hard to get someday. Because someday, gentle manager, is already here.

11

Evaluating People Helpers

I would wager one month's salary that if I could speak with your present supervisor (and if she would be perfectly candid with me) she could tell me a few things about your work performance that could stand improvement—and I mean things you don't already know about. And I would make the bet even if you had received your annual evaluation yesterday.

How can I make such a wager? Because the price of complete honesty is too high and most of us are not in the habit of giving timely and regular feedback on job performance.

And that, of course, is the shame and sham of most annual employee evaluation efforts—we give too little too late. In a way, the annual employee evaluation system encourages our procrastination to avoid what is unpleasant and, unfortunately, the same system helps us put off a much more important function; rewarding staff for work done *when they do it*.

Employees have both a right and a desire to know how they stand with you and the company. They should not have to wait twelve months between feedback sessions. If people with our backgrounds in human behavior do not know the basic principals of reinforcing good behavior and helping people correct unacceptable behavior, who does?

Here is an unfortunate but typical scene from one of those rough meetings with your boss during which you are recommending a staffer be let go.

YOUR BOSS: So you want to terminate Fred. I thought he'd been doing better.

YOU: No, he's made his last mistake. It's a chronic problem with him and I see no hope for his ability to change. He's been this way since the day we hired him.

YOUR BOSS: Let me see his performance evaluations for the last several years.

YOU: Oh, those. Well, I guess I was trying to encourage him.

BOSS: Let me see them.

(Your boss reads through several years of annual evaluations.)

BOSS: Looks to me like you should be promoting Fred, not firing him.

YOU: . . .

Well, I let you make up the excuses.

Too many nice people

In my experience most people-helper managers are just too nice to go around offering their formal and considered opinion on the work of those people who report to them. It just isn't the sort of thing one does. Besides, we ask ourselves as we fall back into our role as counselor or clinician, what do I *really* know about this person who works for me?

Maybe his poor performance is because he's been having trouble at home? Maybe something happened to him back in childhood that made him this way (late for work)? If I'm really candid, maybe he'll blow up and quit? Maybe he'll blow up, quit, and file a lawsuit? And maybe his mother weaned him on a breast of stone and your giving him some honest feedback about what he needs to do to do a better job will cause him to regress and soil himself or become suicidal and end up in a psychiatric hospital.

Sound familiar? It should. Any time we clinicians try to get down to brass tacks with our employees around an evaluation/ performance issue we start experiencing role confusion and, to one degree or another, often wind up in some pretty colorful escape fantasies.

So, to get us out of the Land of Oz and back to plain, old black-and-white Kansas, let me make some suggestions that should help you get this part of your job done with less fear and trembling.

Our Peculiar Backgrounds

First, I think it is helpful to understand your own experience relative to the evaluation process. Anyone reading this book has been evaluated; not once, but thousands and thousands of times. From kindergarten forward our society has been weeding out those around us. A few got weeded out in grade school. Many more got weeded out in high school. Thousands more were weeded out in college. Then came graduate school. The weeding-out process went on, now with a vengeance. Of those starting into college, only a small percentage ever earn a graduate degree.

In case you hadn't thought of this, you and the people who work for you (assuming they are college graduates) represent the precious few. Most of them have been at the head of whatever class they were in since childhood. Sitting around a clinical staff meeting one day it occurred to me that the average IQ in the room at that moment was at least a standard deviation above normal (and probably much higher) which, as I thought about it, was an abnormality in itself.

Bottom line: The people who work for us are smart, they've proved it, but they are *unaccustomed* to receiving negative evaluations.

I remember when I was in graduate school that if a student got a *C* he was considered doomed. Not that he had just received the grade of *C* and was average, but DOOMED. When you get down to the final years of our graduate training in America and have been weeding out the less fit through better than sixteen years of formal evaluations, it is no wonder that we end up with people who are unaccustomed to receiving a grade of less than *A* or *B* or that, when you tell them they are somehow deficient, they pale, begin to quiver, or fly into a rage.

As I once told a personnel director from the world of business, "In mental health, we only hire prima donnas and admirals . . . the rest work somewhere else."

When you combine our training to always be nice and give everyone a second, third, and fourth chance, our experience with more or less constant success ourselves, and our cultural difficulty with complete candor, it is no surprise to me that even our negative evaluations of employees read like letters of recommendation.

The Right Form

To get off on the right foot, it is important to use an evaluation form that makes sense, especially for clinicians and counselors. That's assuming you wish to use a form at all. Some agencies do not use forms and ask that supervisors write up a yearly summary of the employee's strengths, weaknesses, and what he needs to do to improve. I have no quarrel with such an approach, but it assumes that all supervisory people are adept writers and that they are using some sort of shared yardstick. This is usually not the case on both accounts.

Most employers use forms, generally not very good ones. I know of very few employee evaluation forms that everyone likes. Rather than describe any single one in detail, I'll just discuss the dimensions I think are important to evaluating people helpers and maybe you can use these dimensions to devise your own form.

One mistake to avoid is simply to adopt some employee evaluation form from the business world. These forms have to do with courtesy, promptness, productivity, attendance, responsibility, typing speed, quality and quantity of output, etc., and have relatively little to do with the dimensions of behavior and performance that concern a clinician's work. Use one of these standard business forms and your staff will dismiss the importance of the evaluation even quicker.

Here, then, are a list of dimensions you may wish to consider in drafting an employee evaluation form for people helpers. These dimensions were devised by the staff at the Spokane Community Mental Health Center and evolved after several years of working with less-helpful employee evaluation instruments. You may wish to use a five- or seven- or ten-point rating scale on each variable and tag one end with "superior" and the other end with "unsatisfactory." (The language of "commendable," "satisfactory," "marginal" or whatever can be fitted in between these two extremes.)

Quality of Work
- ability to establish and maintain a therapeutic relationship
- ability to handle intense client feelings
- ability to conceptualize problems, diagnoses, and treatment plans
- demonstrates sound judgment in decision making
- work is accurate, timely, neat, and reliable
- work results in attainment of program goals

Quantity of Work
- amount of work and level of productivity

Dependability/Accountability
- extent to which the employee can be depended upon to carry to completion any task assigned
- demonstrates accountability with regard to paperwork, charting, training, keeping supervisor informed, and stays in compliance with procedures manual

Initiative
- the extent of job interest, dedication, and willingness to extend oneself in completing assigned work

Adaptability/Cooperation
- willingness to work for and with others and readiness to adjust and accommodate to changing priorities

Job Knowledge
- a clear understanding of those facts or factors pertinent to all phases of the employee's work

Punctuality/Attendance
- maintains a pattern of regular and prompt attendance

This form should also include a place for the supervisor's written remarks regarding specific strengths and areas that need improvement, and a place for the employee to comment on the evaluation if she so wishes. The form should be signed and dated by both parties.

I might add that such an evaluation form is not adequate for the evaluation of supervisory staff; you need to rate these people on a different set of dimensions. These dimensions might include the following: demonstrates fair and equal treatment, gives feedback to staff in a timely fashion, resolves complaints, follows consistent policies and practices, welcomes suggestions, expresses instructions clearly, motivates staff, meets program goals, etc. Since many agencies overlook the need for a separate set of categories for the rating of supervisory personnel, you might wish to explore the need for such an instrument in your own shop.

The Annual Evaluation Interview

Now that you know all about forms, you can shove them in a desk drawer and forget about them. Because what really matters in being a good manager is learning to give feedback on a regular basis, not just once a year.

If you make it a practice to let the people who work for you know how they're doing at least once a week, their annual evaluation will be neither a pleasant surprise nor a bitter disappointment. What's more, you, your agency, and clients will have benefited from improved performance throughout the entire year, not just in the few weeks that follow the annual evaluation.

Still, and no matter how good you get at giving people feedback, you will probably need to conduct the so-called annual evaluation. Here's how to get the most out of it for you and your staff.

Rule One: Be prepared. Know what points you want to cover in advance, including those that may not be reflected on the form you have completed.

Rule two: Be flexible. If, when filling out the evaluation form, you had some doubts about how to rate an employee on, say, his ability to cooperate with others, you can, during the interview and after you have handed Fred his evaluation, simply say, "You know Fred, you'll see I had some trouble with item 7, the one about cooperation. Could you help me with this?"

Such an honest inquiry on your part can lead to an open and frank discussion of your concerns and can give Fred an opportunity to explain his side of the matter, correct any misperceptions you may have acquired, and otherwise lead to a fruitful outcome.

Rule three: Give yourself plenty of time for the interview. Because of a desire to avoid the whole unpleasantness of employee evaluations, you must resist the temptation to catch someone in the hallway and say, "Have you got a couple of minutes? I need to do your evaluation." Even worse is the practice of dropping the evaluation in the interoffice mail with an attached note that reads, "Any questions? Call me."

Rule four: Give the employee notice of the evaluation meeting with you. You can even ask her to think about what areas the *two* of you might want to discuss. By making it a "we" meeting, you will cut way down on the paranoia.

Rule five: Treat the interview with the same respect you would treat an interview with a client: i.e., hold phone calls, close the door, and allow no interruptions.

Rule six: If you must give someone some negative feedback that produces tears or anger or unacceptable excuses for failures to perform (and you know this might happen), be prepared to exercise your option to refer them for professional help. The annual evaluation should not turn into a therapy session.

Rule seven: If you are going to ask for candid feedback from employees about *your* performance as a supervisor (and many supervisors use this opportunity to get such feedback), make darn sure you know what you're asking for. Too often supervisors say they want feedback, but then behave in ways incongruent with this verbalization.

Talking too much, folding your arms as if to say, "When I want your opinion, I'll beat it out of you," or the glance at the watch that precedes the "Oops, looks like we've run out of time. Heh, heh," are the usual supervisory dodges.

Since staff can only come away from such a session with a bad taste in their mouths and a sense of democracy betrayed, don't bother asking for feedback unless you can take it. It might help to remember that you, just like your staff, are either a prima donna or an admiral and, most likely, no more receptive to negative input than they are.

Lastly, I want to underscore the desirability of reinforcing staff on a frequent and regular basis. It has been my experience that in the world of people helpers we often assume that each of us gets his ego food from a different place than regular people. This is simply not true. Just like everyone else, we like to be stroked for our good work, for a job well done, and for how we help to make our agency a going concern.

We need this stroking from our bosses because, for a variety of reasons, our clients are (and often should be) a poor source of positive feedback for our work. Those we help often move out of our lives quickly and never look back, let alone send us cards and letters about how much they appreciated what we did for them. (Want proof? Look in your desk drawer and add up all those cards and letters testifying to your clinical skill and generous human spirit.)

The more chronically ill or desperate our clients, the less capacity they may have for gratitude. And, in any case, we should not seek all that much payoff from those we serve.

So where do we get our strokes? Our attaboys? Our feeling that we are doing our jobs well and that, when we get up in the morning, we can look in the mirror and see someone who can take care of business and earn his own way in the world?

Salary won't do it. Benefits won't do it. Flexible hours won't do it. Although better than a sharp stick in the eye, even an expensive office with a view won't do it. Colleagues help, but they're never quite enough either. No, where we get that all-important praise is from our supervisor.

Since the desire to be appreciated is at the core of human nature, I can think of no more important job for a manager than to learn how, where, and when to reward staff for the sometimes difficult work they do. With a good, operational reward and feedback system that functions rain or shine, week in and week out, the job of evaluating your staff once a year should be just so much duck soup.

12

A Short Course
on Clinical Supervision

The business of supervising the clinical work of another mental health professional is so complex, so touchy, and
so poorly understood that I hesitate to write this chapter. But
because so few of us ever receive *any* training in how to go about
it, I thought I ought to at least share some of what I have
learned after doing better than twenty years of it. I have also
listed some useful texts on this subject in the bibliography.

In my own training as a clinical psychologist I received not
one single hour of instruction in how to supervise another
therapist, and it was not until after I had been supervising other
clinicians for fifteen years that I attended my first seminar
about how to do it—which is a bit like teaching a flight student
all about landing procedures after he's airborne.

While this absence of training in clinical supervision was
hardly the exception in the graduate schools of the 1960s, it is
my understanding that things are not much different now. And
yet, since you are reading this book, you are, most likely, somehow responsible for not only the quantity of the work done by
your staff, but also the quality of that work. You are, in addition
(and as may be determined by a court of law), also legally liable
for the work of those who report to you.

To raise your anxiety a bit (in order to better grab your
attention) consider for a moment that as a supervisor of clinical
work you may be responsible for any of the following possible
problems: failure to provide the correct diagnosis; failure to

provide the correct treatment; failure to document difficulties in the case; permitting a supervisee to perform services for which she is unqualified; overlooking a medical problem which, had you seen the client yourself, you would have spotted straightaway; allowing an unethical misuse of a patient to occur; failing to deal with a client complaint of discrimination registered with a supervisee who elected not to notify you of the complaint. The list could go on and on, but my point is this: The job of supervising the clinical work of others is serious business and, since the law often interprets the supervisor to be the ultimate authority when things go wrong, a *very* serious business.

This supervision proposition can be even more unnerving when you stop to realize that the great majority of assessment and therapy work is done behind closed doors with no one there to witness what's going on except the client and the clinician. And in your role as a supervisor, the only description you may ever get about exactly what does transpire in those sessions is that which the staff person is willing and able to provide. The whole process can be as aggravating as trying to buy a painting you've never seen; the seller tries his best to describe the hues to you but, unknown to both of you, he is slightly color-blind.

There are, of course, ways to combat this problem: sitting in with a staff person during interviews, videotaping, audiotaping, one-way vision mirrors, and such. And I strongly recommend all of these techniques and approaches to observing and getting at the actual therapeutic behavior of your staff. The trouble is, these approaches are expensive, time consuming, frequently intrusive to clients, sometimes resisted by staff, and, generally, more appropriate to the training setting, not the ongoing, day-to-day clinical setting in which most of us work.

Therefore, my focus in this chapter will not be on the labor-intensive supervision required of beginning professionals, but rather I will try to suggest some general guidelines and tips for the routine management and supervision of the clinical/counseling work of those who report to you. My remarks here are anything but comprehensive and I will apologize beforehand to those readers who have made a career of the teaching, training, and supervision of other clinicians.

I should also note that much of the routine work with clients is done by persons without graduate degrees or any formal training in the theory and practice of counseling and psychotherapy. Case managers, for example, are often trained at the bachelor's level. These folks will frequently need a different level of supervision than that to be discussed here. In my experience, many will need basic training in the concepts and constructs of human growth and development, as well as a theoretical framework from which to understand the personalities with whom they work. Such a discussion is beyond the scope of this book.

Starting Out

Let's assume you have either just been promoted to a supervisory job, or have hired a new staff person, or have had someone transfer to your department. Whatever the circumstance, the arrangement calls for you to supervise this person's clinical work.

Assuming you have some idea about how supervision ought to proceed, I strongly recommend that the first hour between you and a new supervisee not be spent talking about cases, but about supervision per se. Supervision is, after all, a unique relationship. You (the supervisor) are supposed to have "Super" "Vision," i.e., you can see further, clearer, and more accurately than the person reporting to you. (At least that's the theory.)

On the other hand, the supervisee is presumed to be in need of something you have: wisdom, knowledge, guidance, direction, input, support, understanding, whatever. Whether the supervisee actually feels these needs is another matter, but for the moment let's assume he does.

To get off to a good start, it has been my experience that a thorough discussion of the subject of supervision needs to take place. To get things going, you can talk about your own supervision experiences, what sort you received, from whom, what worked, and what didn't work. Thus invited, your supervisee can share her views, her experiences, and what she has found most helpful. This will likely be a sensitive interview since, at base, you are discussing issues of power and control. But in my view, power and control are best talked about now, not later.

This is also a good time to discuss training backgrounds, theoretical orientations, therapy styles, and the like. In a word, get to know each other and how each of you thinks about people, what makes them sick, and what it takes to make them well again.

Since I abhor inefficiency, I use this hour to train a new supervisee about how I like to work, how I want cases presented, reviewed, and so forth. For example, I do not like a supervisee to begin, "I've got this real depressed guy whose wife just left him and he's been drinking for a whole week and I'm worried he might do something." Rather, I train all supervisees to begin, "I have a thirty-eight-year-old, married, caucasian male, assistant professor of Druid Studies who is acutely depressed and has been binge drinking since his wife of twelve years moved out last Thursday . . . ."

I don't know about you, but I want the lay of the clinical land up front, concise, and factual. Family history, test findings, lab reports, medical status—give it to me fast and straight. We can get to formulations, clinical hunches, and such later on. Unless I set the expectations for how I want the data base presented and get this role indoctrination work done early on, we can both end up wasting a lot of time.

In this first hour it is also important to come to some agreement about the goals for supervision. What does the supervisee hope to achieve, to learn? How would she like to grow? What skills does he want to develop? What sorts of clients would he like to work with in order to expand his experience and knowledge base? What weaknesses does she see in her clinical work? What strengths? If she has had countertransference problems with clients in the past, what are these? How were they handled?

Much like a first interview with a new client, these first few hours between you and a supervisee should lead to a sense of mutual understanding, mutual goals, and, most importantly, a sense of trust. Since counseling, psychotherapy, nursing, and people helping in any of its many forms is an intensely personal undertaking, we need, from the very beginning, to establish an atmosphere that says, "for the good of the client, we're in this together."

In some settings it is only in supervision that we truly share with another person how we do what we do, what we feel when we do it, and how our offer of help does not always relieve the sufferer. We are, more than at any other time, exposing the very nature of what we are as human beings, including, and especially, our frailties and fears. If we are treated casually or coldly or with righteous authority while thus exposed, we are unlikely to share our work fully, or learn, or grow, or mature as therapists. Worst of all, our clients will not benefit from what supervision should offer.

Support Your Local Therapist

One of the key jobs of the clinical supervisor is to provide support to her supervisees. An adversary they don't need. It is easy to forget one's own early years in this field and one's first experiences as a novice therapist. But if you will reflect back a moment, my guess is you will quickly recall the near-terror experience of your first patient.

Remember the panic-edged questions that raced through your mind: "If this patient terminates after one session, will they give me an *F* in psychotherapy? If this client fires me, am I unfit to be a therapist? If this person doesn't get better, do I turn in my nursing badge and go into retail sales? *Why oh why* did they give me such a tough first case!?"

I remember one of my first patients (a forty-year-old, recently divorced mother of four admitted voluntarily for the first time to a state hospital). I was conducting the admission interview of this psychotically depressed woman. Weeping and wringing her hands, she pleaded, "Doctor, I can't even remember how to turn on the washing machine. Have you ever had a patient who could not remember how to turn on a washing machine? Have you ever helped anyone as hopeless as me?"

Stuck for an answer and feeling a rising panic at not being

able to reassure the lady honestly, I turned to my supervisor (a senior psychiatrist). He winked at me and told the lady, "Don't worry, Mrs. Smith, lots of people forget how to turn on the washing machine. And, yes, you'll begin to feel better in a day or two. . . ."

Fact: I was *not* a doctor (yet). Fact: I had never met anyone who had forgotten how to turn on a washing machine. Worse, I couldn't remember in which chapter of which text I should have read and remembered the Forgetting How to Wash Syndrome. Fact: I had no idea what the course of this lady's depression was going to be. Fact: I had been working at a psychiatric hospital for a whole week and wasn't even sure in which direction one might find the men's rest room.

That so-called vast clinical experience upon which I could have drawn to help this lady through her admission lay several years ahead, and had it not been for the kind, warm, supportive reassurance given me by my supervisor at that moment I might have spent some sleepless nights wondering why I hadn't taken up forestry as a profession after all.

It is important to be especially supportive of staff when they are dealing with high-risk clients, clients whose relapse rates are high, clients whose behavior presents risks to others and the community at large, and those clients who are ill and approaching the end of life. Suicidal people, the chemically dependent, some of the personality disorders, offender populations, the aged, and the terminally ill come to mind. Certainly there are other groups. But my point here is that while the work is noble, it is also consuming and it's the supervisor's job to care and understand and support the counselor/healer in every way possible.

Teaching

A clinical supervisor teaches—either by modeling how the work is done, telling how it is done, or by directing the learning of the supervisee. As I have said earlier, much of the manager's work is directed to the adult development of his staff, including arranging for pertinent learning experiences.

Very briefly, I have found the following things useful to this process:

- From my files of articles on clinical theory and practice, I will frequently give supervisees important, case-relevant papers to read and suggest that we discuss the author's work at our next session.
- When presented with a tough interview situation where the therapist is having trouble dealing with the client's presentation, I will sometimes assume the client's role, play it out, and try to see what's going wrong. Or I may reverse the roles (have the supervisee role-play his client) and show the supervisee how I might handle the situation.
- I will frequently draw on my now "vast clinical experience" and share similar cases or situations or therapeutic impasses and how they were managed. (This is clearly a graybeard tactic, but if you've been in the field five or more years, you can probably get away with it.)
- If I'm stumped, I will refer the supervisee to someone who is especially good at whatever the problem is so that that someone can provide the proper knowledge and help. I have no qualms whatever about referring a supervisee to someone who has greater knowledge of a subject or type of client or clinical syndrome than I do because, frankly, I gave up pretending to know everything about everything years ago—an attitude whose adoption, by the way, I can highly recommend.
- And sometimes I just confess to a supervisee I don't know what the hell to do. Not counting the times I really don't know what to do, I sometimes say this just to get the staffer going . . . you know, get him sweating creatively to solve some problem or other.

Finally, I feel it is the manager/supervisor's job to direct and plan for specific training events for his supervisees. Such events would include in-house training, external seminars, and even college seminars and courses. To keep a clinician/counselor at maximum effectiveness and always growing, the supervisor needs to encourage (by word, deed, and cash) the continuing intellectual development of those who report to him. When you consider that the half-life of psychological knowledge is now about five years, you can see that this obligation is no small undertaking.

When Things Are Not Working

In my experience, the great majority of supervised clinical work goes smoothly. If you have hired well, your problems will be few. But when something does go wrong, it often goes very, very wrong.

If the clinical work of a staffer remains in a constant state of disrepair (i.e., every other case has something wrong with it), then a new treatment plan is probably in order—for the therapist, not her clients. My operating assumption is that the average client will get better if only given half a chance, and often in spite of his therapist's bunglings. Since the average client is much more forgiving of her therapist's faults and failings than the other way around, I tend to side with clients when a therapist shows a pattern of "problematic" cases.

In no order of importance, here are a few signs and symptoms of supervision that isn't working. Where I can I will suggest some ways to get it working again. (A problem-oriented approach to the subject, this sort of thing comes from being brainwashed by too many years of problem-oriented charting.)

Problem 1: Staff with too many crises.

Let's begin with you. Probably the most common mistake made by clinicians who graduate to the dubious rank of supervisor is that they try to remain the primary therapist for all the patients in their department. For lack of a better term, I will call this the puppeteer approach.

In the puppeteer approach, staff bring you their client's problems and, by pulling this string a little here, and that one a little there, you direct, control, and manipulate the staff person to do exactly what you would do if you *just had the time* to see this patient yourself.

Since you are the one with the vast clinical experience, it is easy to take over the case, tell the staffer what to do, how to do it, and wait for the positive results to pour in. Because it is easy, appears efficient, and seems to make sense, the puppeteer approach is a great temptation.

You generally know you did not resist the temptation when the following data begins to accumulate: staff phone you for solutions at all hours of the day or night; staff stand outside your office door hoping to get in so that you can solve "their" newest problem; staff seem, after a while, to be incapable of handling even the smallest clinical situation.

If you find yourself growing weary of staff coming to you with problems, find yourself resenting their seeming incompetence, and find that no matter how many times you tell them how to do therapy they don't seem to be "getting it," then it's time to look into the mirror.

Solution: Examine your own needs to control the therapy of others and ask yourself the following questions: Are you fearful that if the clients don't receive the benefit of your knowledge and experience, they will not get better? Do you believe your staff are truly incompetent? Have you been such a good-guy problem solver that you have never required of your staff that they think through a problem on their own?

Assuming your people are, in fact, competent, the supervisor must resist the natural temptation to conduct therapy through his staff. To become a puppeteer will not only stunt the growth of those who report to you but it will, in the end, drive you, as the English say, "round the bend." Doing good supervision is like doing good therapy; you supply the seeds to grow apple trees, not the apples. (See the last chapter for more on this subject.)

Problem 2: Cases you never hear about.

Treatment staff, at least in many outpatient settings, will typically carry thirty or forty cases—more or less depending on the nature and type of clients, work-load obligations, and other variables. If you have three or four or seven counselors, it is simply not possible for you, as clinical supervisor, to know all these cases as well as you would like.

Unless instructed otherwise, mature staff will usually select those cases for supervision with which they need help. This is fine. The more mature the counselor (i.e., willing to acknowledge a need for assistance), the better this casual system will work. This is as it should be and there is nothing wrong with this approach so long as one proviso is always met: that the staffer always knows when he needs help. This is a very large proviso.

Over the years I have noticed that when something goes wrong with a case, it is usually a case the supervisor never heard about. This is such a routine phenomenon that some time ago I drafted the following Law of Clinical Entropy: It is the undiscussed case that disintegrates first.

On later review of a problem case, one usually finds one of two reasons why the case was never brought up for supervision. First, the therapist's feelings toward the client were confused or ambivalent or hostile or (too often) overly affectionate, and (consciously or unconsciously) the therapist avoided the needed frank discussion of the countertransference problem.

The second reason a case might not be brought up for review is that the therapist simply failed to assess the severity of the situation or the ongoing issues in his work with the client properly and was lulled into complacency. A missed diagnosis, a missed communication, an overestimate of the client's strengths . . . any number of judgment calls can be in error. Also, as staff often have too many clients to worry about and too little time to see them in, fortuitous between-session events can sometimes overtake the best-laid treatment plan and a crisis will result.

Solution: To minimize the effects of the law of clinical entropy, you and each of your staff keep a running list of all active cases. (A computer may be able to supply this list.) With this list in hand at each supervisory meeting, discuss the pressing problems first, then review, each time, one or more of the cases that seem to be going well.

You will learn two things: what the therapist is doing right with some cases (for which you can stroke the therapist), and what may be going not-so-right with others. The point here is to have no "undiscussed" cases and, hopefully, no surprises.

You might also keep in mind that you are, in fact, responsible for the ultimate welfare of those clients seen by your staff. Therefore, if a client needed a neurological consult, or a revision in his diagnosis, or a letter of documentation regarding his legal status, or any of a host of other administrative or clinical services, you are the one on the hook to see to it that the work was done and not overlooked. According to my attorney friends in the world of torts, the law refers to this sort of sloppy supervision as malpractice.

Problem 3: Staff whose clients never seem to get better.

By "never get better" I'm not referring to those patients whose mental illness is chronic and whose anticipated length of stay is indefinite; I'm referring to that great volume of clients whose counseling or psychotherapy should, depending on your school of thought and training, take considerably less than a lifetime.

(A proponent of brief therapy, I should confess right off that my views here are essentially that people should get just enough therapy to solve the problem they came in with, keep it solved, and no more. Depending on circumstances and client characteristics, this can take one session, three sessions, twenty-five sessions, or five years. But if the client comes back for even one visit that the *therapist* needed, then it was one visit too many.)

For reasons of which they are rarely aware, some therapists do not accept new clients, they take captives. This problem is not always obvious until you begin to study the therapist's readmission rate (how many people keep coming back for a little more help), how long her average client stays in counseling compared to other therapists in the same program, and how resistant she is to supervisory suggestions that maybe she should move her clients faster, set clearer therapy goals or length-of-stay expectations with her new clients, or that, by terminating people sooner, she could help some of those desperate people on the waiting list.

Solution: Assuming that there is some urgency to work effectively and efficiently with clients and that we are not talking about elective psychotherapy, and further assuming mild confrontation, review of her caseload with particular and frank discussion of possible countertransference problems does not lead to positive changes, then, it seems to me, you have only a couple of choices left.

One, you recognize that you are about to take the supervisee on as a therapy client yourself (to get the change you feel is necessary), or, two, you ask that the therapist seek therapy herself.

In the first instance, I do not think it fair or wise to begin to treat a supervisee for what may be a core problem she has in working with clients, unless it is very clear to both of you that that is now the contract between you, i.e., me therapist, you patient. You're not being paid to be her therapist and she may resent your efforts. Worse, she may take her countertransference problems deeper underground. This is good for no one—least of all the clients for whom the two of you are mutually responsible.

In most settings asking that the staffer seek professional help for his countertransference problem makes the most sense. Although it is not an easy task to accomplish, when patient welfare is at stake, I see no other alternative.

In-service educational efforts, reading of pertinent professional literature, setting program expectations for length of stay, and case status reviews should all help as well.

Problem 4: Staff member cannot seem to keep clients.

Especially with beginning counselors, you may notice a high no-show rate for second or third appointments and a series of precipitous terminations from treatment. (Intake appointments—because the client has not yet met the therapist—are not affected.)

What is happening is fairly clear; clients don't like Joe and vote with their feet. Something is happening in those first visits that is off-putting and your job is to find out what it is. And quickly. Clients will forgive therapists' failings to a point, but they are not saints.

For example, I once inherited a counselor from another department and while he was a likable enough chap, he talked too much. When his no-show rate jumped up after first appointments, I got to wondering if he talked too much in his intake sessions with new clients. I called one of his early dropouts. The lady confirmed my suspicions: "Oh, I liked Mr. Smith just fine. But I couldn't get a word in edgewise. I think he should be in sales."

At other times the therapist may trigger premature terminations by binding the client's anxiety, looking or acting helpless (thus diminishing hope even further in a hope-seeking client and causing him to look elsewhere), or by otherwise muffing the initial interview by minimizing the client's complaint, acting disinterested, or moving too fast into panic-laden material.

Solution: To stop premature terminations, directly observe or tape the staffer's interviews. The problems should be obvious. As clients who drop out when they still need help are often the best barometer of a therapist's effectiveness in building a working relationship, don't hesitate to talk to them. Surveys requiring a written response will net you about a third of the candor a phone call will. In my view, the client is generally right and as clinical supervisor it is our job to find out what's going wrong and to fix it—including reassigning a disappointed client to a new therapist.

Having been involved in training many therapists over the years, it has been my experience that the student is often only slightly less anxious than the client they've been assigned to see and that, if you get hold of this dropout problem quickly, you can get things back on track in short order.

With more mature therapists the problem is more than beginner anxiety or lack of skill, thus requiring a more thoughtful and careful approach. Sometimes a clinician is so fed up and burned out with people helping that his nonverbal communication is as follows: "Yes, you've got a problem. Yes, I'm a therapist. But in case you haven't noticed by my attitude and posture, I'm too pooped to care. So would you mind taking your problem to someone who gives a damn?"

This problem, as you can see, requires a serious intervention, a referral for therapy, or some kind of reinvigoration of the staff person.

Problem 5: Therapy/counseling not working.

Only an idiot would undertake to recommend solutions for why a client's treatment may not be working. But being at least part of a fool, I'm going to list some of the signs and symptoms and suggestive implications for a therapeutic effort that may be failing or that needs supervisory attention. Excluding issues of medication (a subject about which I'm not qualified to comment), these indicators may be detected in the supervisee's presentation of his cases to you. As a result, you can direct your queries and concerns to those cases in which these signs appear.

- As already discussed, any cases that seem to have been deselected for review.
- Cases where there seems to be a lack of focus. While this rambling confusion is obvious on a video or audio tape, it is difficult to detect from a retrospective verbal presentation of the session. However, even the therapist's best efforts to attribute purpose, meaning, and clarity to a session where none was present usually won't wash.
- Difficulty moving forward by rehashing issues already discussed. For example, the therapist and client agreed long ago that the client's mother was a cold witch, but they also seem to have agreed to rehash the temperature requirements for witches through an endless series of weekly appointments.
- Client complaints or expressions of dissatisfaction. Since clients only complain about their treatment reluctantly, I take all such complaints seriously. Frequently missed appointments are often a clear indication of client dissatisfaction.
- The therapist is dissatisfied with the client. For example, the therapist is chronically late for his appointments with Clarence. Recommendations for premature termination, inappropriate transfers to group therapy, or any expression of anger or hostility toward a client in a supervisory session may indicate the treatment relationship is failing.
- The therapist seems confused about a case and has trouble telling you exactly what is happening in the sessions. Gail simply cannot articulate the processes, dynamics, and patterns of interaction between her and her client. Often this is a countertransference problem.
- Overpersonalization of the client's problem. Therapist remarks that "This guy's a real creep" or "I can't believe the way this woman acts out!" are, again, probable countertransference issues.

- The therapist cannot clearly state the goals of therapy. This usually results from defocusing by the client, secondary-gain maneuvers by the client, or outright manipulation of the therapist by a client more clever than the therapist. (It happens.)

Solution to all of the above: While there is no simple or single formula for solving the problems that may be triggering these signs that therapy is not working (and the list, by the way, is hardly exhaustive), I think that to do a good job we have to be aware first of the many impasses and problems encountered by our staff in their work with clients.

But to be able to be made aware of these problems requires a high-quality relationship and an open atmosphere with our supervisees, which, in my view, is our job to establish and maintain. Sharing supervision problems with other supervisors, attending seminars on supervision, and improving one's supervisory skills should also help, but it is the quality of the relationship between us and those we supervise that will best minimize problems for our shared clients.

In this regard, I might add that any time things go wrong, it is important to take the problem apart in little pieces and, in a kind of microanalysis of the issues, reconstruct the history of the mess, carefully examine what happened, and then to move into new areas of candor and understanding between you and your supervisee. Such an analysis will often prove the patient (the easiest person to blame since he or she is not present) did nothing wrong and that the fault was ours—which brings me to one of my final points.

Any time you find yourself ganging up with a staff person against a client (and you can usually feel your blood pressure rise during the consultation), you'd better back off and examine what is happening very, very carefully. You may be perfectly correct to be as upset as your staff person about the patient's behavior, but you may also be perfectly wrong in the decision you are about to make.

Too often I've seen inexperienced clinical supervisors fed misinformation, limited information, distorted information, and the occasional outright lie so that a staffer can justify some punitive action toward a client who has angered or frightened him. Desirous of supporting staff at all times and especially when they are upset, supervisors can occasionally be deluded into a bad move. Therefore, strongly worded recommendations for precipitous terminations, refusals to readmit, sudden transfers or forced hospitalizations (always for the "patient's own good"), need to be carefully reviewed with a cool head, a disinterested third party, or a colleague who has no stake in the outcome.

A Few Final Observations

If I am supervising someone in the early phases of his professional development I feel my obligations to him are greater than just keeping him and his clients out of trouble. The mixture of supervision to clinical work should be rich, multimodal, and highly educational for the trainee. I usually tell such supervisees that we have a pilot-copilot relationship; they're flying the plane, but in case of an emergency, I can choose to take over. However, I will do so only if and when I feel the client's welfare is imperiled. This relationship is carefully explained to each client we "share." Rarely do I have to take over the controls.

With staff whom I have supervised for many years, the mixture of supervision time to clinical work is much leaner, so lean, in some cases, that for all intents and purposes, the staff person is operating as a solo practitioner. But I am still there, still willing to help, and still have an obligation to be the backup pilot in case something goes wrong.

In anticipation of some questions you may have, let me answer them quickly and get this chapter finished.

- Yes, I think supervisors should continue to see clients. You may have earned your spurs years ago, but to maintain credibility as a clinical supervisor, you can't keep quoting that "similar" case you worked with back during the Nixon administration.
- Yes, I think doing dual therapy with supervisees is desirable provided, of course, you don't run the whole show.

- No, I do not think all therapists can work with all clients. This supposition is absurd on the face of it and, as a supervisor, you should never ask a therapist to work with a client who causes him to feel revulsion. And vice versa for clients.
- Yes, where possible it is a great luxury to match clients to therapists so as to maximize "fit" and, hopefully, therapy benefits.
- Yes, I think clinical supervisors should be promoted from the field (combat promotions) because a supervisor with no clinical experience with clients is generally worse than no supervisor at all.
- Yes, separating one's other management obligations from those of one's job as clinical supervisor is sometimes difficult. But it is by no means impossible. By letting ethics be your guide and keeping the client's welfare first in mind, your duties should fall into place.
- Yes, there are many cultural/minority/ethnic issues in therapy that require (at the least) consultation or training from specialists sensitive to the limitations and contexts in which therapy must occur. Where the hearing impaired are concerned, this is even more critical.
- No, I do not believe one profession is better than another at this business of clinical supervision. If anything, the dominance of the medical profession in our field is a historical and legal artifact and says nothing about competence to train, teach, or mentor the counseling, social, or psychotherapeutic work that most of us do.
- Yes, I consider clinical supervision a matter of continuing education for all practitioners and, to the degree necessary to provide quality care, feel that *everyone* doing clinical work needs a supervisor.
- Yes, I consider gender differences between therapists and clients and supervisors a potential source of sex bias and sex role stereotyping that needs and warrants complete candor in the supervisory relationship.

One final comment. Whether in a training institution or in the field, I personally feel that the unique and highly charged work of therapy and clinical supervision is not enabled or ennobled by a sexual relationship between a supervisor and a supervisee. At best, confusion reigns; at worst, the supervisee is exploited, the supervisor rendered ineffective and the client's interests obscured and neglected.

13

Managing Stress

Given that you are already a professional in the area of human behavior and may know more about the subject of stress than I do, I'm going to take a nuts-and-bolts approach to stress with emphasis on what you, as a manager, can do about it. Basically, I'm going to suggest some specific things you might consider doing to reduce stress in your workplace, in your staff, and in yourself.

Since you already know that optimum levels of stress maximize performance while too much impairs it, I'm going to skip all the theory and focus on reducing what I will assume may be too-high levels at your place of business.

Stress in the Workplace

You already know that so-called stress-related illnesses are on the rise. Employers everywhere are alarmed about the growing number of psychological disorders that experts argue are the direct result of certain occupational requirements. Based on the stress/risk characteristics of their work, paramedics, policemen, firemen, and others are filing more and more successful claims for mental and physical disorders that result from their work. And many experts feel this is only the tip of the iceberg.

In general, jobs that can be described as having the characteristics of high demand coupled with low control (clerks, waiters, fry cooks, etc.) are seen to contain the essential ingredients of a stress-producing situation and, therefore, such jobs are viewed as partly responsible for the stress-related illnesses these people suffer.

When you consider that suits for psychological damages caused by purely psychological injuries (e.g., sexual harassment) are increasingly successful and that more and more courts are agreeing that there are powerful and hurtful effects from strictly psychological stimuli, it ought to give us managers in the human service industry pause.

For example, what psychological difference is there between sexual harassment and the kind of harassment staff complain about when a patient singles them out for late night phone calls or follows them home after work or threatens to injure them or their families? What difference is there between a hospital attendant working with an angry and potentially assaultive patient and the policeman who brought the patient to the hospital? What difference is there between having upset clients sent to your office for counseling and the cook who has no control over the orders sent to him? Are these not similar high-demand/low-control situations?

Question: When will mental health, nursing, counseling, and other human service professionals begin to file lawsuits claiming that the nature of the work they do is the proximal cause of their psychological damages?

My hope is that this never happens. But the pessimist in me says that the day of stress-related disability claims and lawsuits from people helpers is coming and that, to the degree it is possible, we managers need to be prepared for it.

But there is more to it than our just avoiding disability claims or lawsuits. We need healthy, high-functioning staff if we are to get our jobs done well and see to it that the mission of our agency is achieved. No one can be of any help to a client if he is off sick. Therapeutic effectiveness hinges on staff who are healthy, positive, and experiencing those optimal levels of stress that peak and inspire maximum performance.

In my view, the first order of business for managers is to realize that the client can only come first when we have taken good care of ourselves, our work environment, and our staff. And while I may be preaching to the saved, many Fortune 500 companies are convinced that the management of stress is so important to the bottom line that they have and are developing comprehensive programs to reduce stress and increase the hardiness of their employees, especially their managers.

Here, then, are a few things you might wish to consider relative to reducing stress in your workplace, most of which, by the way, have to do with increasing the control experienced by staff rather than reducing the demands upon them:

- Spend some time and money to make your work site look and feel pleasant. Too often when I go into a public mental health center or counseling agency or pastoral counseling setting, what I see are dingy, dimly lit waiting rooms that were furnished with someone's hand-me-downs and, frankly speaking, are more depressing than the people sitting in them.

However you can do it, the place you work should say, "Hope lives here!" Bright fresh paint, a few flowers and plants, paintings and positive colors and themes—these are things that communicate how an agency feels about itself. And for Pete's sake, have a smiling, sincere, helpful receptionist!

There is more here than just appearances; we owe our clients the respect a pleasant, warm, clean work site speaks to them. We owe them a decent setting in which to struggle with their problems.

And there is something equally important; we owe our staff the same sort of environment. As much as can reasonably be afforded, a work site should get the same care and attention you would spend on buying a new mattress for your bed. You'll be spending about eight hours in each, so don't go cheap.

- Since noise is a major stressor, take whatever measures are necessary to reduce it: sound proof counseling-room doors, carpet the floors, cut down on street noise, etc. If you don't have one already, acquire a phone system that allows staff to control incoming calls, route them elsewhere while they are with clients, and otherwise enables them to maximize their control of this odious electronic intruder.

Phones are the epitome of the high-demand/low-control stress-inducer, especially when you consider the kinds of phone calls most of us get. With very few exceptions, people only call us when they have a problem, are in trouble (usually serious trouble), have a complaint, or are experiencing some acute emergency. If you get one call in a hundred where the person says, "Gee, Tom, I just called to say thanks for being such a help the other day . . . it really made a difference in my life," You're batting way above average.

- Set up a health awareness committee. Given the proper task assignment and authority, this committee can give staff a chance to develop health-promoting programs for all employees—diet classes, exercise classes, recreational outings, fun and games. Once under-way, the committee only needs to meet occasionally to work up new ideas and keep the established programs going.

At my own agency, some of the nursing staff have volunteered to provide free blood-pressure checks several times each year; other staff lead classes on nutrition, weight control, aerobics, and, while it took some doing through education and leadership, our work environment and atmosphere now speak "health" to anyone who enters them.

Considering the costs of obesity, smoking, alcohol abuse, hypertension, underexercise, and other risk factors that affect our staff and their ability to be on the job and working at a hundred-percent efficiency, it is only good sense and good economics to support and encourage them to avoid these lifestyle diseases. As managers interested in reducing stress in the workplace and keeping our work force healthy and *able* to work, we must push for this kind of programming. Like that great guru of physical fitness Mickey Spillane once said, "If you don't take care of your body, where are you going to live?"

- Reduce fear and/or risk of injury. One of the chief fears of mental health workers is of being physically assaulted by clients. We don't like to imagine it happening, but it does happen and staff worry about it. Administrators often minimize staff concerns in this area and resist taking the measures necessary to reduce this source of stress, partly for reasons of cost and partly because no system is going to be so perfect as to prevent all risk of assault. Still (and if your agency deals with this sort of client) there are some fairly inexpensive things that can be done.

First, establish a procedure for handling clients who are out of control. Such a procedure usually calls for a show of numbers to discourage the client's further acting out. Practice this procedure until everyone feels that he is not alone in his office or on the ward in the event something begins to happen. Special training in this area is available as well.

Next, if you have counselors in individual offices, consider some of the low-cost alert systems that can be activated by the counselor pushing a button at her desk. Such systems may notify the telephone people that help is needed and where, or it may trigger a not-too-intrusive external alarm (usually mounted somewhere in the hallway) that will summon nearby staff to the office where the help is needed.

You may never need to activate such a system (and frankly they are a lot of bother for what is a low-probability event) but they do send an important psychological message to staff: We care about you. Such systems also give staff (again) a bit more control over their environment, or at least that equally important *sense* of control over possible events.

- It may not be possible in your shop, but wherever it is possible, try to give staff control over their own schedules. This may include the particular clients they see, when they will see them, and the hours they work. I am aware of the efficiencies of central scheduling and the necessity for staff to see people they would sometimes as soon not see, but the more you can let them set the parameters around the work they do (hours, appointment times, etc.) you will again be permitting them to have some mastery over their professional time and will help maximize their feeling of being "in control"—thus reducing their experience of stress.

You as Stressor

You may not know it, but it is at least possible you may be causing stress in your staff—maybe just enough, but maybe too much.

For a moment, let's assume that I was able to get your staff into a confidential conversation about you. What would they tell me about you and the stress you produce in them? For example, do they experience a twinge of fear when you come into a room? Are they made anxious when you send them a memo to increase productivity or reduce errors? Do they go home at night and rage to their spouse about what a miserable, rotten, capricious, arbitrary egomaniac you are? Do they go to see their physician and say of their headaches or ulcer or hypertension, "If you worked for the same bastard I do, you'd have symptoms too." Do they ever take a sick day, not because they are tired of seeing clients, but because they are tired of seeing you?

Well of course none of this could be true about you or me, but we both know managers who do this to people for a living, don't we?

Penetrating question: Is it possible you are a so-called toxic boss? Some stress experts argue that managers are the carriers of toxic stress and that, possibly more than any other factor, it is the manager's management-effect on his staff that accounts for most of the *distress* among those who report to him.

But are we not supposed to cause a little stress? Are we not supposed to raise the tension level a bit so as to maximize performance? The answer is yes. But how do we cause just enough stress to get perfect performance levels from our staff without frying them, putting them on the sick list, or causing them to resign. (This is the $64 million question. If I knew the answer I'd be writing this paragraph to you from a hot tub in Malibu.)

Reducing Your Toxicity to Staff

The following suggestions are based strictly on my personal experience and observations of managers and are, therefore, unencumbered by any scientific findings or controlled research. At best the product of literary license, these observations may be dismissed out of hand.

First, however, you might consider a couple of things: You are probably not aware of the stress you are causing your staff and, most everything I've read or experienced suggests that the so-called difficult boss accounts for about 20 percent of the stress workers experience while at work.

In no order of priority, here are a few tips:

• Get untangled from your staff.

To reduce perceived stress caused by you, you must begin to separate yourself socially from those who work for you. This is difficult to do, but you may have already noticed that since you became a boss, you get invited to fewer and fewer staff parties. It is a warm and wonderful feeling to be considered "just one of the staff," but, in fact, once they start paying you to manage your colleagues, you just ain't one of 'em anymore. And if you don't know this separation has begun, your staff certainly do.

Too often managers try to be both coworker and boss and, failing to notice or accept the short but significant distance between themselves and those who report to them, they often make a mess of things for everyone concerned. They do this by mixing their requests for performance with appeals to a pal, by giving wishy-washy orders for the same reasons, by hedging on their expectations, and by trying to stay on a best-of-friends basis with the people through whom their job and the mission of the agency must be achieved. While some managers may be able to pull this off, most cannot.

This awkward positioning can lead to being manipulated by some staff ("How can you ask me to do this? Don't you re-member, you had chicken at my house?"), to being resented by others ("Ha! He didn't ask Mary to do this job because he had chicken at her house last Saturday"), to being considered stupid by still others ("What kind of an ignoramous would have chicken at Mary's house and let himself get compromised so that he can't be fair to all of us?").

Now imagine the mess you will create for yourself if you should *sleep* with Mary (and it gets around).

This business of social intimacy is a sticky one and much harder to deal with in rural areas where the social structure does not permit one to withdraw from roles so easily. Still, some role distinction is essential to your functioning as a manager.

Consider, for example, the unofficial party at a staffer's house. On showing up you may think you have hung your leadership role in the closet along with your coat, but you will be mistaken. As the boss you are always at risk of being misinterpreted by someone. What you think is a harmless, candid, and casual comment may, if wrongly interpreted, get around the whole staff the next day as gospel. It is sad but true that while you may wish you were officially off duty at one of these let-your-hair-down parties, at least some of the staff won't even let you take your hat off.

Question: Why ruin a perfectly good party for someone just by showing up?

For my part, I stopped putting a damper on staff parties years ago. I just begged off and, with a few exceptions, put together another social life.

• Give up the "big happy family" fantasy.

What I want, a manager thinks to herself, is for my staff to be just one big happy family—then we'll all get along just ducky.

Wherever this need to create the alleged tranquility and comfort of a "family" atmosphere at the office came from, I don't know. Maybe it has something to do with our need for everyone to feel happy, safe, secure, and that they are a part of something great and enduring and wonderful. This idea of being a part of something wonderful is fine, but to frame the quest in family terms is, in my opinion, both naive and dangerous.

First, if you've done any amount of family therapy, you should know right off what an impossible dream perfect family tranquility is. Second, any time a manager promises to create, maintain, and nurture a network of relationships as complex as those that accrue in family life, she has taken on a task more formidable than a space launch. Third, since someone has to be Mommy and Daddy, who is this person? You? And if you are Mom or Dad, what does that make your staff?

Finally, because of the nomadic nature of the American

worker (and especially those in our field) the "office family" is, perforce, constantly suffering grievous loss through relocation, retirement, promotions, and people quitting for better salaries and benefits. Among other dissimilarities, families don't split up for "better money."

To avoid or reduce stress among your staff, don't ask them to join a family; ask them to do a day's work for a day's pay and to get along with each other as professionals whose common purpose is superb patient care. If they happen to make some good friends along the way (including you) that's fine. But as for building one big happy family? Forget it.

- Don't even try to avoid conflict.

From the epigrammatic pen: Staff conflict is not only unavoidable, but is absolutely unavoidable.

A manager's job is not to try to duck, eliminate, or expunge any suggestion of conflict among his staff, but rather to manage it. To not manage conflict (or pretend none exists) is to let conflict run out of control and, possibly, result in unnecessary stress to your staff.

On more occasions than I care to remember, one staff member has come to me to complain about the interpersonal behavior of another staffer. So long as the complaint had no basis in actions that were unethical or illegal and the parties were coequals on the same team, my reply has always been, "You are two adults, you are both trained in communication and problem-solving techniques. It is my strong recommendation that if you have a problem with Fred, you need to talk directly to the person who can do you the most good."

"Fred?"

"You got it."

In almost every instance this approach to managing staff conflict has led to positive resolution and, I must assume, less festering, long-term stress between the parties involved. Occasionally a conflict-mediation session is necessary between staff, but only rarely. And certainly this approach has caused me less stress—no small consideration for a manager who wants to remain as nontoxic as possible.

Unless you like counseling staff with personal conflicts between them, I'd suggest you step back, encourage them to act like responsible adults, and learn to work around and through their differences—otherwise you may find yourself refereeing a fight where the only loser will be you.

Final note: To the degree a manager perceives her staff to be "children who need proper parenting" she will be forever undone by her staff's infantile behavior—at least some of which she may be sponsoring by her own style of dealing with subordinates. (More of this in a later chapter.)

• Be scrupulously fair.

If there is any one thing that will demoralize staff, cause them sleepless nights, fits of anger, and homicidal fantasies in which you are the central figure, it is the perception that, when it comes to dealing with your staff, you are UNFAIR.

It goes by many names—nepotism, prejudice, bias, favoritism, inequity, and frank injustice—but by any name it smells the same. Even a whiff of unfairness can undo the morale and psychological well-being of your staff; a chronic case of it can ruin the efforts of your whole department and imperil the mission of your agency.

Of course it is easy for me to say that so long as you always do the right thing at the right time and in the right way and are always perfectly on balance with all of your decisions, you will cause less stress among your staff. But that is exactly what I am saying we must all strive to do. And if you haven't yet achieved this level of leadership, then I hope you can bank on ignorance and inexperience. Because whereas staff will forgive stupidity, they will never forgive intentional injustice.

Here, then, is what to keep in mind: *Any* decision that affects *one* staff member has the potential to affect *all* staff members. Therefore, to minimize the amount of toxic stress you cause your staff, all you have to do is never make one of these poorly thought-out decisions that can possibly be perceived as unfair, now or in some foreseeable future.

To never make a bad decision you will need the vision of a prophet, the IQ of a rocket scientist, and the wisdom of Solomon—or pretty much your standard manager equipment package. But if you somehow got into your present job by faking these basic credentials, then you will probably screw up once in a while. Just try not to make a habit of it and never, I say *never*, be unfair on purpose. It's the "on purpose" part of an unfair decision that brings down everything from CEOs to governments.

• Send fewer memos.

Of all the forms of risky communication humans have invented, the office memo ranks right up there with brandishing clubs and war paint. Memorandums, unless they contain nothing of import, almost always carry and cause stress. Usually sent to prevent conflict, they more often cause it.

To reduce levels of toxic stress caused by memos, consider the following points:

1. Never send a memo that contains controversial material. The recipient, unable to ask questions or reply, has to stew in his own juices until a meeting is held to sort out what the hell the memo really meant.

2. Get editorial help with any memo that has even *the slightest chance* of being misread or misinterpreted. Find your best writer/communicator, put your own author ego in the drawer where it belongs, and get some help with the language. If a memo can't be understood by the average sixth grader on a first reading, it shouldn't be sent.

3. If you get an angry memo from someone (the modern-day equivalent of throwing the first stone) do not reply in kind. Call them up, go see them, whatever . . . just don't start a war with the Xerox machines.

4. After you have dated, initialed, and are ready to send a memo, stop, give yourself a couple of minutes to consider other ways to communicate the same information, and then, if the memo does not have to go out that instant, put it to one side and send it tomorrow. A better form of communication might come to you.

(The cure for memo-itis, by the way, is to dig out all the memos you sent last year and carefully reread them. It's a pretty rough cure, but every manager ought to take it once in a while.)

5. If an important bit of information (policy change, benefit change, proceedural change, etc.) must be sent by memo to gain full distribution and uniform clarity, prepare staff for the arrival of the memo by discussing it with them in advance, either personally or in a meeting. You will knock down no end of confusion, distress, questions, and anger if you just let people know something new and different is in the wind and that it will be arriving by memo.

What people really seem to hate about memos is that they are always a one-way communication, no one is handy to interpret what they mean and, as a result, no one seems interested in their reaction to the content.

. . . end of memo lecture.

- Never ask staff to do something that is patently wasteful of their time.

A major source of stress in any agency is paperwork. Not just any paperwork, but that paperwork which staff consider useless and wasteful of their time. Forms, like dandelions, seem to spring up in every agency. Researchers need forms filled out, reviewers need documents completed, computers need numbers, millions of numbers. It seems the need for documentation is endless.

To my mind, there are at least two ways to keep forms and useless paperwork to a minimum: Charge some group like the quality assurance committee with the responsibility to review the utility and value of any new form or paper request, and/or attach a dollar cost to the time it takes staff to complete some possibly nonessential piece of paperwork. If there is no compelling reason for the paperwork, drop the requirement like a hot potato.

If you stop to consider the cost in dollars or stress (often the same thing) for any request of staff, it will make such decisions much easier, and will greatly reduce the distress that people feel when "Someone is wasting my time!"

Of course the best remedy for all new forms and such is to

have the executive director fill one out; this process will kill off about 90 percent of the nonsense before it ever gets started.

- Never personalize a criticism of a staff member.

This sounds like an obvious thing not to do, but because we are human and sometimes upset (and because upset humans say and do things they regret) managers sometimes attack a worker's self-esteem. "You never do anything right!" "Hell, man, are you incompetent, or what?" "You blew it, *again*."

It doesn't matter if the staffer was incompetent, did make a mistake, or really screwed up—what matters is that we not destroy her sense of well-being, personal pride, and feeling of integrity. What we need to do is to reframe criticism as an adult learning situation so that the person can accept our request for change or our observation that she made a mistake and shouldn't make the same one again. But we don't need to cut her throat or strike her firmly about the head, shoulders, and ego.

If you are ever tempted to fall into the win-lose dynamic of setting up situations wherein, because of your greater administrative power, management always wins and staff always loses, try to remember *Stalag 17* and how the prisoners undid their keepers. And if one day you begin to feel as frustrated with your staff as Colonel Klink did with his POWs, maybe you will need to sit down and have a long talk with yourself about how power really works.

In my own view, and within the civil context and delicate fabric of human service organizations, attempts to "win" through the exercise of raw power always precede losing—and what is lost is always much more than anyone thought was at contest.

Reducing Your Own Stress

I have already said much of what I think is important about how to manage your own stress on the job. If you reduce all the environmental stress you can, reduce the stress you may be causing your staff by being a better manager (there is nothing more stress inducing for the manager than a stressed-out staff), and avoid such things as borrowing trouble by trying to solve interpersonal problems between the consenting adults who report to you, then you should feel less stress yourself. This is called, I think, enlighted self-interest; you take care of yourself while you are taking care of business.

I might remind you that as one of the high-priced staff, you are not supposed to be throwing yourself onto the bayonets and under the tanks. Unless you want to volunteer to become a test case for managerial burnout, I'd strongly recommend you take care of yourself, stay healthy, and continue to set that shining example of mental and physical well-being to which your staff can aspire.

Having worked over the years with many managers who became, as they say, "stress cases" I'm still not sure what it takes to manage one's own personal, work-related stress. There are dozens of stress-reducing therapies, biofeedback, relaxation methods, yoga, long walks on empty beaches, you name it, everything seems to work at least some of the time for some of the people. Since there must be at least as many ways to reduce one's stress as there are to save one's soul, I'm in no position to recommend one over the other.

But let me say a brief word about what I call toxic jobs.

In my opinion, there are some jobs that are undoable. By that I mean that given person A's values, work habits, and personal standards, she simply cannot do job B without suffering high and harmful levels of stress.

For example, not long ago I was working with an RN who had recently accepted the director of nursing service (DSN) position in a nursing home. The nursing home had been poorly administered, was in deep financial trouble, had hired a great many people who were incompetent, unreliable, irresponsible, and, as a result, many of her staff were not fit to provide patient care. Personnel problems were rampant, staff morale was too low to measure, and patients were suffering (and occasionally dying) from negligence. To top things off, the chief administrator couldn't be bothered with all these "little" problems that the DSN was supposed to take care of.

Enter my client. Full of goodwill, bearing the highest standards of her profession, and ready to right the wrongs of the long-term care system, fix up this particular nursing home, and provide the best treatment and services possible to the patients under her care, she set about what might be considered an impossible, if not toxic, job.

At first it took fifty hours a week to get on top of the problems. Then sixty hours a week. Then seventy. Then her best charge nurse quit. Then another patient died due to probable staff negligence and failure to follow procedures. Then she was told she could not fire anyone that needed firing because it would lower staff/patient ratios and endanger certification and medicare payments. She was told she would "just have to make do" and try to contain the contagion of incompetence. Our heroine (my client) hung on.

For a while. For a few months.

Then came the sleeplessness, the nightmares, the questioning of her career choice, the anxiety, the depression, the weight loss, and so on down the list.

Point of story: Managers can do a great many difficult things and work long hours and sweat out the tough decisions and still keep their stress within normal limits. But what they can't seem to do is compromise their values, their ethics, or their sense of obligation to those for whom they have vowed the best possible care. Or if they do, they may become physically or mentally sick or both. Worse, they may become the Nurse Ratched of *One Flew over the Cuckoo's Nest* fame—uncaring, cold, distant, and inhumane.

Unhappily, I have seen a few managers evolve into this Nurse Ratched kind of flat-eyed bloodless bureaucrat. With so little passion for their work and so little kindness left in their hearts, it makes you wonder how such people can look at themselves squarely in a mirror or cash their paychecks.

But I'm riding off on my charger here, so let me finish up by asking you a couple of questions about your job: Is it doable? Is it possible for you to get done the things that must be done to accomplish your mission of care or counseling or service? Are the decisions you make in keeping with your principals, values, and beliefs? Given that we all must stretch and give a little and force-fit things once in a while, are you engaged in so much of these acrobatics that you have to assume more and more unnatural professional positions?

If your answer to these questions is uncertain or causes you a troubled feeling, then maybe you owe it to yourself to spend some time examining what's happening with you and your job. Talk things over with a pal, share your concerns with your boss (she needs to know things are not well and can't do a thing to help if she doesn't know), or even see a therapist. But don't become one of the Pod People (bloodless bureaucrats) or a Nurse Ratched or get sick and quit the human service field. We need good people, especially good managers.

Lastly, I have a rule that I like to share with staff from time to time, or when some onerous chore needs doing, and I especially share it with new staff. You might find it helpful.

I tell staff that while I expect them to work hard and to deliver the goods, I will never ask them to do something for which they are not qualified, or that is unethical, or that I would not do myself. More, I tell them that it is their responsibility to tell me if I am about to break my own rule.

This simple assurance to staff seems to carry our relationship a good way. It says to them that our work together will not be confused or clouded by any demands from me that they compromise their professional values or sense of what is right and wrong for our clients. Maybe it is only a matter of setting the tone for the work we do, but to me it is a pleasant and proper tone that permits high trust and goodwill—two of the most powerful antidotes for what some might consider a high-stress occupation.

14

An Inward Look

Whatever else we think of our work as managers, I believe all of us owe ourselves a moment of introspection. Maybe two moments. This chapter is written to encourage you to take a bit of time for what might prove to be a helpful self-examination.

What follows here are mostly personal observations based on my clinical and counseling work with managers from the human service field. Based on this experience, I am quite convinced that we managers create at least some of the problems with which we struggle, and that these problems are ones that we personally carry to the job, not something inherent in the work itself. As we may have said or thought about a client, "Charlie is his own worst enemy," I think the same interpretation sometimes applies to us.

The Little Therapist Who Could

Based on formal and informal surveys in my own agency and judging from the reports of others, there appears to be an unusually high number of adult children of alcoholics among the people-helping professions—quite possibly over 50 percent of us, and some say the percentage is even higher. Some of them are recovering people, others have grown up in alcoholic families but never became chemically dependent themselves. No better protected than the general population, many of us grew up in nonalcoholic but otherwise dysfunctional families. We may have been victims of physical or sexual abuse, or maybe psychological neglect or overprotection. Maybe we suffered the loss of a parent through divorce, desertion, or death during our formative years. Since no one escapes childhood emotionally unblemished (and regardless of your school of thought about family of origin and childhood influences on adult functioning) there remains little doubt that how we function as adults and managers reflects, at least in part, what we learned during our formative years.

Having worked in therapy with all sorts of managers (including many from our own professions), I can safely say that much of what I have read in the general business management literature about the common failings and errors made by folks in the world of manufacturing, finance, and business are due precisely to those attitudes, beliefs, and habitual ways of thinking, feeling, and acting that one acquired as a child. To the degree these attitudes, beliefs, and habits are dysfunctional, you will have an ineffective manager.

For example, let's consider the Little Therapist Who Could. In an oversimplified dynamic, many of the people-helping managers I have worked with were the "little therapists" in their own disturbed families of origin. From the chemical dependency literature, this role is often referred to as the "Hero." Having failed to save a parent or brother or sister from themselves or the slings and arrows of outrageous drink, these people developed powerful needs to be competent and to control others and, so the theory goes, grew up to study religion, psychology, nursing, social work, medicine, or some other healing art in order, as I've interpreted from my client's histories, to be able to finally "get it right."

The operational hypothesis of the Little Therapist Who Could seems to be: If you try hard enough, never make a mistake, and do it all yourself, you will finally succeed.

But to have any chance at all, you first need perfect control. And to get perfect control you need authority and power—which is why, according to some, otherwise-capable clinicians and counselors eventually apply for jobs as managers.

The Hero's work habits reflect this try-try-try attitude and his guilt over perceived failure to perform is legend. Perfect control, unfortunately, comes only at a very dear price. Ulcers, for example. Or alcoholism. Or a kind of fuming angry depression over having too much work to do and never enough competent help. In the managerial training seminars from the business world you will see the problem reflected in such management self-analysis questions as the following:

- Am I uncomfortable if I have nothing to do?
- Do I have to take work home every night?
- Do I work longer hours than those I supervise?
- Am I frequently interrupted because others come to me with questions and work-related problems and decisions?
- Do I spend some of my time doing things for others which they could do for themselves?

The list goes on. Answer yes to these kinds of questions and, rather clearly, the manager has a problem with delegation.

Question: Is this failure to delegate the result of lack of skill or understanding of the principles of good management, or is it, rather, that the manager's inability to let go and let grow has something to do with emotional decisions made in childhood?

It has been my observation that, as children, many managers were pushed into surrogate parent roles while still very young and long before they were emotionally ready for such responsibilities. Now, finally given the power to "take care of people," such a manager's failure to delegate cripples his effectiveness.

My speculation here is shored up by my experience that while you can send staff to management-training seminars until the cows come home, more often than not you will be disappointed in how little behavioral change you see back on the job. Is something else at work here?

Of the many examples of how our unmet childhood needs and or experiences can influence us in our roles as managers, let me share a personal example.

Dr. Marshmallow, I Presume?

One of the well-known errors managers frequently make is to condone incompetence or failure to perform. We know an employee is working far below her known potential and yet, out of a fear or need we cannot even name, we fail to act, confront, or otherwise deal with the situation in a timely manner. Our apparent need for the approval and admiration of others (or maybe the fear that someone "won't like us") overrides our responsibilities as manager.

Early on in my career as a manager I so needed this love and positive regard from my staff that I earned the dubious title of "Dr. Marshmallow." Dr. Marshmallow was a patsy. With a vulnerability that could be spotted across a crowded room, Dr. Softy avoided confronting staff when they needed it and, as a result, frequently got had. Not once, but many, many times. Too nice for my own good, I traded acceptance for responsibility and habitually made allowances where none were warranted. Into the bargain I rationalized my actions, slept fitfully, and built up a considerable stockpile of resentment toward those people who seemed to be taking advantage of my kindness.

It took me a long time to forego "love" and settle for respect. Believe me, respect is better. Not only do you sleep better, but you do a better job for your agency, your staff, and your clients.

Prone to introspection and wondering where this vulnerability came from, I was able to find the roots of it in my own childhood. Working this through with someone else was a big help.

Are We Codependent?

If you will allow me to further speculate about how our management responsibilities might be influenced by the possibilities of our own emotional issues and how these issues may be reflected in our management decisions, let me suggest to you that the literature of codependency may have something to say to all of us. This literature, as you know, comes to us from the world of alcoholism and chemical dependency and attempts to describe the roles, attitudes, beliefs, and behaviors with which children emerge from their dysfunctional families.

Whether or not this literature will survive the research it needs is not material for the moment, because what I am about to say in this chapter is intended to be provocative, not final; food for thought, not the dessert.

As you know (and even though the term has been overused

and misused a great deal lately), an enabler is the person in the alcoholic's life who inadvertently assists the addict to continue using his drug of choice. Enablers are nice people—tolerant, forgiving, kind, and, unaware of the true needs of the person with whom they are dealing, remain ignorant of their role in perpetuating the addict's addiction. An example is the boss who unknowingly forgives the alcoholic employee's falling face first into the punch bowl at the Christmas party every year.

The codependent, like the enabler, does this and more. Often a relative by blood or marriage, the codependent picks the alcoholic up when he is down, bails him out of jail, gives him money, may even buy his favorite brand of bourbon when he's hung over or celebrating a birthday, and, as a consequence, suffers within the relationship as much or more than the identified addict. The relationship endures, month after month, year after year until, standing back to study what's going on, you begin to see that the codependent needs the relationship (however pathological) as much as the addict and that both need outside help.

In the broadest sense, a codependent does for you what you should be able to do for yourself. Some feel a codependent is any person whose life has been adversely affected by a long-term relationship with someone who is highly dysfunctional by reason of chronic illness, chemical dependency, or some other debilitated or impoverished physical or mental condition.

Mind you there is nothing wrong with being helpful to people who need help or who cannot help themselves. Dependency is healthy, natural, and something we have all been, and, unless we die suddenly, are likely to be again. Dependency, at least in my view, becomes problematic only when it is no longer appropriate to one's developmental stage in life or level of personal competence.

For example, you can tie a two-year-old's shoes. You can help a four-year-old tie his shoes. But if you insist on tying a ten-year-old's shoes (and he hasn't learned how because of your constant attention to his needs), then he is now pathologically dependent and you are the codependent. Since the boy is now dysfunctional and the mother (at some level of awareness) realizes this, neither can separate from the other because, obviously, you can't expect a boy to go out and face the world if he "can't even tie his own shoes."

In an advanced state, the codependent bends over backward to help, worries about others until she is sick, fears to trust her own feelings, and says yes instead of no when no was clearly what was needed. She may even get sick worrying about caring about those who can probably care for themselves.

You may be wondering, what has all this to do with me? Bear with me, I'm getting there.

Let's assume that at least a few of us have codependent traits (and by the way, I'm not sure they will let you into human service work without them). As clinicians, counselors, and people helpers, we like to be liked. We like to solve problems, especially other people's problems. We like it when people come to us for advice and help. Compared to the rest of the world, we are even willing to go to the person with a problem. Healers at heart, we would do everything we could for someone down on his luck. Isn't that what this work is all about?

Yes. And there is nothing wrong helping those who cannot help themselves. But what if they *can* help themselves? And what happens to a strongly codependent people-helping professional who works his way into a position of power and authority? What happens to his needs to control others so that perfect outcomes can be attained and all anxiety over uncertainty vanquished?

Hypothesis from the epigrammatic pen: Staff who are dependent in unhealthy ways will become positively dysfunctional under a codependent supervisor. And, contrariwise, staff who are *not* dependent in unhealthy ways will resent the dickens out of the manager who insists on tying their shoes for them.

If you're a trained therapist, then you have already learned how not to create and encourage unhealthy dependency in your clients or patients. You've learned to keep the client reaching, moving, trying new ways of being. You've learned to not do for someone what he can learn to do for himself because you know, in your therapist's wisdom, that you will stunt and stop your client's growth if you take over those functions and responsibilities that are truly his.

Question: Have you applied this same wisdom to your staff?

Or have you, as some of my manager therapy clients have done, failed to distinguish between being a helpful boss and being a codependent one?

When you consider that even if you personally do not have codependency issues mixed in with your management role, some of your staff most assuredly will, then maybe what follows will be helpful.

Common Codependent Mistakes

In no order of importance, here is my hypothetical list of managerial errors that, in keeping with the speculative nature of this chapter, may have something do with those attitudes, beliefs, and behaviors we acquired as children and that, even as mature adults, may be influencing our leadership style. In no order of importance, I have lumped them under the rubric of codependent mistakes, but I imagine other theoretical language could couch it just as well. And there are surely more.

1. The failure to develop your staff.

If my supposition about codependent managers is true (that we need people to need us *excessively*), then it follows that we will tend to do for staff what they should be able to do for themselves. Why? Because maybe they will like us *even more*.

As an example, you know you're making this mistake when you simply *must* call the office a couple of times a day while you're away at, say, a workshop.

Message to staff (and with love): "I can't leave you guys alone for even a day, can I?"

Interpretations by staff: "The boss must think we're incompetent if he has to call us three times a day." "The boss is an overcontrolling SOB." "The boss really cares about us, but he doesn't trust us for one minute."

My reasoning here is that the manager calls the office frequently while away because, momentarily not in perfect control, his anxiety drives him to it. His staff are probably the last thing from anxious. In fact, they are probably the most relaxed they've been in weeks.

If you find yourself thinking of your staff as somehow helpless, hapless, needy, and unable to function without you (and objectively this is not the case), then you are likely to develop an unspoken operational policy that reads, "Don't do anything on your own that I haven't previously approved." Like a totalitarian government, this unwritten policy essentially stops all creative problem solving, all decision making in your absence and instills a dependent/codependent working relationship.

Since I've already covered the absolute necessity to develop staff elsewhere, I won't rehash it here. I'm only suggesting that our reasons for failing to do so may say more about our childhood decisions than about what we learned in our last management-training seminar.

Also, such an attitude about staff will often taint hiring decisions; you just hire people who come to the interview with their emotional shoes untied.

2. Using the *they* word.

Much as the codependent mother blindly defends the helpless son whose shoes she must tie every morning, so the codependent manager would defend her staff against a cruel administration. Both use the *they* word.

MOTHER *(about the school, etc.):* They don't understand him. They question my love for him. They are thoughtless and unfeeling.

MANAGER *(about administration):* They are insensitive to staff needs. They demand too much. They don't understand how hard we work down here.

As soon as you hear a manager use the word *they* instead of the agency *we,* you know you have a manager headed for deep trouble. Not only will the manager drive a wedge between himself and his agency, he will encourage even more unhealthy staff dependency. As he steps into the role of parent-protector against a harsh administration, he automatically puts the very people he is obliged to serve at risk of being seen as mutineers.

3. The *unfair* word.

There is nothing wrong with the word *unfair*—unless, of course, a manager uses it to describe some decision, policy, or action by the agency that employs him. Policies may be wrongheaded, arbitrary, ill-conceived, and just plain dumb, but seldom are they purposely intended to be unfair.

Unfair suggests someone in authority is taking advantage of little people by treating folks differently. *Unfair* suggests some parentlike figure has pets and favorites. *Unfair* implies you can't trust the administration (of which you are a part) to be just, impartial, equitable, and balanced.

To the degree this prejudiced belief springs from one's childhood experiences, the manager has a problem that is not inherent in the job, but inherent in his attitudinal makeup. Is it not the Hero's job to set things aright? (This is not to deny, of course, that some agencies *are* run by scoundrels and need fixing.)

I have seen many stupid administrative decisions and, to confess a thing here, have made dozens myself. If they upset people it was because they were shortsighted, not because they were maliciously designed to hurt people. But the manager who uses the word *unfair* to describe his agency's decision making, like the manager who uses the *they* word, is headed, more or less directly, into a very fine mess indeed. Stepping into the role of Hero, the manager rears up on the wrong side of the issue and will generally suffer quite predictable and often painful consequences.

(I should note here that throughout this book I have been kind in my description of upper management and CEOs. Wise, benevolent, just, intelligent, good-looking, I suppose I consider myself a member of this august group—which may have something to do with the bias here apparent. But CEOs, chairpersons of the board, program directors, hospital administrators, pastors, priests, or prelates—none are immune from my observations about codependency and its possible implications for leadership.)

4. Giving staff too much slack.

An expert in this area, let me just say that being a really nice person and all-round good guy despite grievous provocation will almost always enable one's staff to continue to act out problematic behavior on the job. Abuse of the agency's trust and goodwill is the common symptom of this dysfunctional relationship between a manager and his staff. Drinking, drug abuse, excessive absenteeism, failures to produce, tardiness, chronic complaining, lousy paperwork, or any of a dozen self-defeating, self-destructive, or system-abusing behavior will persist as long as Dr. Marshmallow is at the helm.

Here are some examples of how to make this mistake:

- Do not confront people about repeatedly coming to work late.
- Do not require that all the paperwork be done.
- Allow Tom to use sick leave to work a second job because, don't you know, "Tom has terrible needs right now."
- Let Clara fudge on her mileage reimbursement because, in case no one knew or cared, "Clara's husband is alcoholic and doesn't bring in a thin dime."
- Make up elaborate excuses for failures to perform, when simple confrontation and swift use of reinforcements would solve the problem.
- Let the normal supervision hour slide into a personal therapy hour. (While a bit of private life may spill over into the supervision hour, there can be too much of a good thing.)
- If staff cannot make up reasonable excuses for why they don't do their job right, you make them up for them.

The list goes on and on. Mind you, this misplaced kindness has to be patterned and chronic before we jump to conclusions about its meaning as a managerial error. But any time a manager has a tacit agreement with a staffer that she can get away with things the rest of the staff cannot, you have an unhealthy dependent/codependent relationship that is at cross-purposes to the agency's needs for responsible, mature employee behavior.

The key ingredient, as I see it, is the manager's position and attitude of overarching sympathy for all his "special" people. In fact, when I hear a manager making excuses for a nonperforming staffer who is one of his "very special people," I get a very certain feeling that something quite unhealthy is afoot.

5. Give till you're angry.

Managers who insist on picking up the heavy end of the board have always bothered me a little. I don't mind the manager who likes to pitch in and help out when he's able, but I've come to distrust the person who just can't do enough for me or the agency. The superhelper who comes at me with the big "Here, let-me-do-that-for-you smile" causes a shiver to run up my spine. Not because I won't appreciate the help, but because I can't see the price tag.

For lack of a more precise term, I'll just call such managers TGTBT (too good to be true). What sort of codependency this might be, I'm not sure.

The too-good-to-be-true manager is just that—he's the one who leaps in to solve all the problems before people even know they have them. Working overtime is his specialty, working weekends is his delight. Ask this manager for a little input and he's up nights for a week drafting you a comprehensive battle plan. With a high need to please others and a driven, almost desperate quality to do the work of those around him, he appears the perfect employee.

Maybe this is the workaholic whose anxiety over not being constantly helpful compels him to such heights of productivity. Or maybe it is the kid who never learned it was okay to take a day off and go fishing. I don't really know. But I do know what happens when such a manager expects his staff to behave in the same, high-minded, self-sacrificial fashion.

Except for the odd true believer who will follow in his footsteps, most staff simply step aside and let such a manager continue his personal crusade to bring solutions to problems and light into the world. This lack of staff response to the TGTBT manager's style seems to inspire even harder work, more self-sacrifice, and greater devotion to duty. Why? Because "someone has to be responsible around here!"

This is all just dandy and as you watch the superresponsible manager skip lunches, take on more and more problems, put in longer and longer hours, you pause to wish that every manager could be equally motivated. With ten like him, you could do the work of a thousand.

But then, one day and out of the blue, the too-good-to-be-true manager resigns. Generally in anger. And, as it turns out, he *was* too good to be true.

What went wrong?

Here's my theory. While the TGTBT manager may report

being only "a little disappointed" that her staff don't seem to have the same energies for the cause she does, she is, at the same time, building a slow, ever-growing reservoir of resentment toward the very people she is trying to lead. Out of touch with the true sources of her anger, she quietly blames her superiors as well. No one, it seems, appreciates her dedication.

Laboring alone in the vineyards day after day, putting in the long thankless hours, sacrificing one's home life for the good of the mission, the codependent, too-good-to-be-true manager eventually cashes it all in with a resignation. Often a sudden, unexpected one.

This is truly a tragedy and a loss, not only for the manager involved, but for the agency, the staff, and the clients. In my experience, some of the most dedicated, most knowledgeable, most compassionate, and caring of all human service professionals fall into this category of being too good to be true. Neither malignant nor willfully malicious, they are apparently blindsided by their own painful childhood experiences and, as a result, seem helpless to alter their leadership style or to sustain themselves over the long haul. Even sadder, they are often miserable, angry people who do not enjoy life.

Having seen many of these managers come and go in agencies with which I have been affiliated, and having counseled many more, I do not believe the codependent, too-good-to-be-true manager can, unless helped with psychotherapy or careful supervision, save herself from an eventual raging, angry flameout. The reservoirs of feeling, you see, are being filled with high-octane resentment.

Such managers will last in a new job about two years, maybe three. If they are working with untrained or marginally trained staff (e.g., a nursing home) where they have to take on even more responsibility for those who report to them, then they might last only eighteen months. But sooner or later they burn out and move on to another job, usually quitting in a fit of temper over some little thing that, on the face of it, wasn't worth quitting a job for.

As a supervisor of a TGTBT staffer (and if you want them around for the long haul) I believe you owe it to them to help them understand that, as the poet says, "too much charity turns the heart to stone." Counsel them in supervision or send them to therapy, but for the sake of your agency and its mission, don't let them burn themselves out.

I might be wrong about this codependency business and am fairly certain my list of managerial errors and their sources in childhood is far from complete. But of one thing I am fairly certain: the consequences of parenting your staff when you have codependent traits has serious consequences for you and your agency. In the short term such an arrangement may work for a while, but eventually the same parent-child struggle will begin and end, unfortunately, with the usual and customary painful consequences.

Here, in my experience, are the usual scenarios of how the struggle ends. These endings, by the way, are seldom in anyone's best interests.

- The manager whose department has been a model for bad morale because of her preferential treatment of her "pets" and "special people" is eventually complained about by other staff until her own performance is found wanting and she is pressured to move on. This crisis is usually triggered only after there have been resignations by the healthier, more independent staff.
- If the manager is not asked to leave or to get help with her codependent style of managing (because her boss is giving *her* slack?) and the healthy people all move on, the department will begin to withdraw and isolate itself from the rest of the agency. Becoming an exclusive "family" within the greater organization, the barriers go up and its participation in the broader mission will diminish until, one day, you have a little shop within the big shop that operates on different norms, different work rules, different procedures, etc. Internal conflict is kept "in the family" and staff are taught never to complain or appeal to higher authority. There is usually resistance to requests for change from the outside by this manager (he's protecting his family) and plenty of tension between this department and others with whom they must work.

Such managers are seldom team players (you can't trust people not to take advantage of you). To survive, such a manager has to outmanipulate everyone else.

- The worst outcome of the struggle occurs when such a manager decides to go to the mat over some issue or other (usually to defend one or more staff who now refuse to tie their own shoes) and, feeling the need of numbers, openly enlists his staff in a holy war against his own agency—the dreaded *they*. Public statements, circulating petitions, contacting a union organizer in a nonunion shop—all of these are precursors to this worst-case scenario. Retreat for everyone becomes impossible.

Failing the efforts of pointed supervision or a therapy referral to help the manager with her leadership style, the only cure for such a dysfunctional family work group is radical surgery, beginning with a headectomy. Transfers don't work. Or if they do seem to work, the fix won't hold. You've just transferred the same codependent manager to another place where she will begin to shape her new staff into the sort of people she must have to satisfy her own unexamined needs. As a result of the transfer, you will also probably lose some of the good staff for whom she has now become responsible, thus losing all around.

Probably the greatest ongoing cost of this sort of managerial leadership (not counting its effect on the clients and mission) is in the rapid turnover of people who hire on not knowing the true arrangements. After a few weeks or months, they smell out the favoritism, the special arrangements, the rule bending, the excuse making for "special people" and they start putting in for transfers or looking for another job outside the agency. At approximately 30 percent of gross salary for the first year of employment going to orientation and training of new staff, the cost of this high turnover rate is staggering.

A final observation.

While it may be wild speculation on my part, I sometimes wonder if the attrition, so-called burnout, and high turnover of otherwise perfectly good, highly trained human service staff can be explained in part by this business of codependency.

Having worked with many of these managers as therapy clients, I have little doubt that the majority of their on-the-job stresses and strains, complaints, dissastisfactions, and grief are, more or less, the direct result of their never having learned to care for themselves. Too busy rescuing others, denying their own anger, disappointment, need for caring and nurturance, and trying to control an imperfect world filled with imperfect people, they come, one day, to feel victimized, unappreciated, and furious. In a word, they get sick or mad or quit. Sometimes all three.

And the saddest part is that the journey never ends. Like the woman who marries one alcoholic after another, the codependent manager takes a new job somewhere else in human services and starts the whole pattern all over again.

Until I had been in this field for several years, I did not think it entirely necessary for therapists and counselors and managers to have had some personal therapy or shared group work or focused supervision on those family-of-origin issues that might affect the way we treat our clients or the kinds of decisions we make as leaders. Well, you can't be right about everything.

At the very least I feel we owe ourselves the time to look inward and to gain the sort of awareness that frees us to make new, more healthy decisions for ourselves, our families, and the people with whom we work.

Finally, about one thing I am increasingly pleased. More and more these days I see managers in our field learning to take better care of themselves. They're eating better, exercising more, giving up their addictions, investing in their family life, and taking their vacations. When I first started out in this business I used to see managers lose vacation days rather than use them. Assuming they were so indispensable to their agencies that they could not afford to be gone even for a single day, the only roses they seemed able to smell were those sent to them while they were sojourning in a hospital.

But this attitude of indispensability and self-neglect seems to be changing. For the better. And in my view not a minute too soon. After all, our agencies, staff, and clients need us not for the sprint, but for the marathon.

15

The Challenge

This chapter was something of an afterthought. Having read a good deal about management in preparation for writing this book, it occurred to me that while many of the authors covered most of the things I have tried to cover here (but without the special application to clinicians and counselors), only rarely did any of them attempt to challenge the reader directly about her motives, predispositions, and "fit" into the role of manager, particularly as that fit may apply to the manager's organization.

Writing this chapter was then, like the last one, something of the work of the old professor-psychologist in me; you know, you've got your listener this far along, so why not indulge yourself a bit and abuse him just a little? At any rate, what I hope to do here is to get you thinking and, maybe, challenge you to be the best manager you can be.

Are You Sweating in the Right Shop?

As I'm sure you know, organizations vary in their nature, purpose, and structure. It is well-known by now that certain people fit best into certain kinds of organizations, fairly well into other kinds of organizations, and not at all into still others. For example, manager A may work out very well in agency B, but he will do very poorly in agency C—not because there is something "wrong" with A's personality or with C's environment, but because A's attitudes, values, social, and power needs are at odds with the atmosphere and structure of C's organization.

Since many managers never seem to quite grasp the company line or feel at home with their agency's social organization, leadership, and power arrangements, this person-to-agency fit is of more than academic interest. Having experienced the top-down authoritarian structure of the US Army, a psychiatric hospital, and a few other organizations, I can safely say I would not be a happy camper working for an outfit like, say, General Motors. And GM, I'm sure, would feel the same way about me.

Without getting too far afield here, let me pose a question: Are you a round peg in a square hole? Are you the type of person who fits well, works well, and gets along well in your type of organization? Since the effective manager must share the mission, goals, and purpose of her organization, this is a serious question.

For example, if you work for a state-run human service organization with a long operational history, a clear power structure and a hierarchy that runs all the way to the state-house, you are probably working in the kind of organization where directions flow from the top down (not the same thing, by the way, as divine guidance).

Top-down organizations have lots of work rules, governing laws and regulations, built-in rewards and punishments, and typically demand a high degree of compliance to detailed procedures. Deviations from authority and established ways of doing things are punished; risk taking is largely discouraged—until, of course, you reach the higher levels of administration, at which time your creativity is both encouraged and rewarded.

With years of bureaucratic evolution behind them, old, top-down organizations typically require you to work your way up to a point where you have the power and authority to be creative and, more importantly, to influence how things will be done. For lots of reasons, some of us haven't the patience for this sort of long march to leadership.

A second kind of organization is that which characterizes many young mental health centers, health maintenance organizations, clinics, and most of the new agencies that have sprung up to meet the needs of our ever-changing health and mental care system. These are small, young agencies where decisions are made via discussion, consensus building, and usually unwritten agreements. Control is not so much from on high, but based on interpersonal influence, commitments to common goals and a sharing of power based on what "we" think and feel. There is usually a management "team" (as opposed to a single all-powerful leader who calls all the shots), but it is not a true democracy in that formal votes are not taken. Since to one degree or another everyone is a peer to everyone else (and therefore included in the "in" group) building and reaching consensus is critical to smooth functioning.

Given that most clinicians and counselors place a high value on self-actualization and hold egalitarian values, this small, flat organizational type would seem to be the most desirable one in which to work. You put a very able bunch of people together in what appears to be a highly professional atmosphere, give everyone an opportunity to have input into how things are going to be, and then everyone can, theoretically "do his own thing."

On the surface this appears to be the ideal work environment. A kind of Camelot for people-helping professionals, I think this is the sort of agency most of us imagine we would like to work for. It is the sort of organization into which we feel we might best fit. But having worked in an organization that grew from a handful of dedicated professionals to a staff of almost three hundred (not counting students and volunteers), I'd like to share a couple observations from that journey.

First, if your outfit is quite small, peopled with bright happy folks who all respect one another's opinion perfectly and no one is tainted by power needs or suffers from the occasional bright idea, then you may, indeed, have found a good organization/manager fit, if that was what you were looking for. The primary ingredient for success of these kinds of organizations seems to be size and stability of top leadership. Small size, close working conditions, personal relationships, face-to-face methods of communication and influence—these seem to be the magic ingredients. For some, this is the perfect place to work.

The only problem is that, except for rural areas where the tax base and population won't support growth, the best "little" organizations have a nasty habit of getting bigger. Success breeds success and, with it, the agency begins to expand and undergoes sometimes painful growth spurts.

Once an agency's staff exceeds twenty or so, greater and greater organization is required for smooth functioning. Greater organization begets more work rules, more formal reporting relationships, more procedures, more codification, more written this and written that. Every time a staffer screws up, a new rule has to be written to forbid the same screwup happening again. Parenthetically, it has always seemed to me that once a work group grows larger than, say, the size of the tribal organizations of our ancient ancestors (about twenty-five souls), we humans begin to get uppity and start writing laws to bother each other.

Here's a second observation. Having worked as a manager in both of these kinds of organizations (large and formal and small and collegial), let me just say that if I want a sheaf of poetry I will hire the small organization; but if I have to fly to New York, I want the plane built by the big guys.

As an aside, Peter Druker, the guru of managers the world over, makes an interesting observation about those of us who would like to "do our own thing" and the kind of organizational structure in which this kind of freedom can truly take place. Basically, he says that only within the context of a strict hierarchy (wherein the roles are carefully defined from top to bottom) is such "freedom" possible. Only where your role is clearly delimited and fully protected by definition of function, tradition, and law, are you free to experiment within that role. For example, at least on the job, a parish priest has enormous latitude to solve problems as he sees fit. And the highest authority of his organization (the pope) cannot enter his church to conduct a mass without being specifically invited.

Interestingly, it seems the oldest organizations (universities, churches, the military) permit the most autonomy, at least with respect to the specifics of how a particular job is done. My college professor friends (and despite their constant railing at the powers that be) have enormous freedom to carry out their duties to teach, consult, and conduct research. Just hint that you might wish them to do the bidding of the administration for purposes at odds with their own academic interests and, judging from the shrieks and howls, you would think you had clapped them into irons and tossed them into prison.

Without digressing further, let me just suggest that since I have seen some very able people make themselves very miserable by working for the wrong organization, I think you owe it to yourself to examine how well you fit into yours. If it's a bad fit, it's not necessarily anyone's fault—but you're the one who will probably have to fix it. Having supervised and counseled managers whose skills were good but whose need for structure or direction (or lack of structure and direction) was quite at odds with those of their employing organization, I can safely say that finding this fit or comfort zone is much more important to one's mental health than one's paycheck.

Leadership

Let's assume for the moment that you are a round peg in a round hole, like your job and the people around you, and enjoy being an active member of the management team.

Question: Has it occurred to you that those who report to you consider you their leader?

Leader!? I thought this book was about management, not leadership. Another question: Where do you get off thinking you know anything about how to *lead* people?

Let me digress again.

During World War II an older friend of mine was promoted from the rank of second lieutenant to that of lieutenant colonel in less than a year. A combat navigator in a bomber over Germany during the height of the daylight American raids, Bill survived his twenty-five missions and, because of the terrible losses among officers and men, arrived at a position of seniority with considerable authority. Later, at the end of the war, this high rank was riffed back and Bill began the Korean War as a captain.

I tell this story because, most likely, you have arrived at your position of manager/leader as a result of a battlefield promotion, not because you went to the mental health equivalent of a West Point in preparation for your job or, for that matter, because you had a burning desire to lead others into the war on human suffering.

While I am sure that you applied for the job you now hold and wanted it because you thought you could be even more helpful, the fact is that many of us are promoted on the basis of a little ambition and a lot of rank—i.e, our academic degrees boosted us into positions of power.

Maybe you were the only nurse around to take the responsibility for the LPNs. Or since your were the pastor, you got to be responsible for the work of the counselors. Or being a PhD, it was determined that you could easily supervise a half-dozen master's level therapists. The first MSW to take on a new project, you are now adding staff to help you with its success. An MD? Shoot! . . . delivering a couple of milion dollars worth of human services through a staff of fifty professionals and support people shouldn't be any sweat—after all, didn't they teach you how to deliver human babies back in medical school?

My point is this: At least a few of us became leaders/managers for some fairly obscure reasons, not the least of which may be that we happened to be in the right place at the right time with the right degree. Except for the money and prestige and the fact that Mom and Dad are proud that we finally earned a title, many of us are unwilling to openly acknowledge our needs to take charge and see to it that something is done in a better, more efficient manner—in a word, LEAD.

Lead, Follow, or Get out of the Way!

I saw the above command on a bumper sticker, liked it, and have now figured out how to work it into this book.

Except for those few managers who, early in their careers, set out to take the reins of leadership by earning degrees in business or public health administration, or who sought special classes in personnel procedures, budget and finance, or who took the time to seek out and pay for seminars and certificate programs in social work administration, grantsmanship, accounting, board development, or what have you, the great majority of us remain ill-equipped to lead through the strength such background preparation would provide. Rather, most of us lead by our wits.

Over time and with good luck, our natural problem-solving skills, above-average IQs, hard work, and levelheadednes may gradually earn the respect of others. We may even develop a dash of charisma. And even though our perception of self may remain that of "only a supervisor" others may begin to treat us as if we were leaders, as in, "show us the way."

Some have argued that the term *manager* is a wimpy term and that people don't want to be managed, they want to be lead. United Technologies Corporation of Hartford, Connecticut, published a message in the *Wall Street Journal* to this effect, asking the following:

"Whoever heard of a world manager? World Leader, yes. Educational leader. Political leader. Religious leader. Scout leader. Community leader. Labor leader. Business leader. They lead. They don't manage. The carrot always wins over the stick. Ask your horse. You can *lead* your horse to water, but you can't *manage* him to drink. If you want to manage somebody, manage yourself. Do that well and you'll be ready to stop managing. And start leading."

I like this statement because it brings into focus a point I have tried to make throughout this book; that to be a successful manager, you must first *manage yourself.* And to do this, you must understand how you tick, what motivates you, and what keeps your juices flowing. You must be savvy about people, power, politics, pundits, and pea brains. You must know if you're sweating in the right shop for the right cause. And as I suggested in the last chapter, you need to know if your leadership style and methods are stress inducing to your staff. Without this self-knowledge you may never become a stress case yourself, but you could, like Typhoid Mary, become a carrier.

Because I personally believe there is a need for all of us to achieve some level of emotional wisdom about ourselves as managers of other people, I feel we could all benefit from a critical self-analysis, a personal study—if not for ourselves, then for those clients and staff to and for whom we are responsible.

People are counting on us. Those above and below us expect us to have all our ducks lined up. Our boss may tolerate an occasional honest mistake, but never habitually stupid ones.

Our staff expect us to know things they don't, to be more experienced, more cautious, more thinking, and more reflective. More mature, if you will. If they expect us to take risks, they do not want us to be brash. If they expect us to be firm and fair to everyone, they hope we will not be rigid when it comes to their request. They want us to place unmitigated trust in them but, as soon as a ripple appears on the frequently troubled waters of managing an agency, at least some will withdraw this trust from us and the rest of the evil "they" of administration.

Because we have to make decisions for the greatest good for the greatest number we will, I think, always be at the center of conflict, the target of criticism, and sometimes the butt of a hushed hallway joke. Being a leader means to earn our fair share of nitpickers and detractors from the ranks of the short-sighted.

But we will also earn the respect of those who recognize our efforts to be fair, firm, and honest in our dealings with everyone.

This is as it should be. This is what leadership is all about.

If you have heard the saying, "It's lonely at the top," and you are in midmanagement, then you also know "It's not exactly a party halfway up either." But that is okay, too. That's what we get paid for, that's where we get a chance to try—maybe to fail, but maybe to win.

In my own view even the smallest, collegial organization needs the best leadership it can get, and at every level in the organization. It is a false assumption that anyone near the top can lead equally well. The boss, the CEO, the one at the top is special . . . otherwise she wouldn't be there.

Oh, maybe when the sun is shining and the auditors and regulators are on vacation and the fees are rolling in and the staff are perfectly content with their salaries and benefits and the clients are all grateful and getting better and not hiring lawyers to sue you into bankruptcy and the competition has folded its tents and moved away and the funding sources have agreed you are the only people who should ever get the grant monies forever and ever, then, maybe, any old leader will do.

But short of this idyllic happenstance, every organization needs a leader, even the two- or three-person office. This boss has to make decisions; sometimes with lots of input and in a measured, cautious, consensus-building manner, at other times quickly, by himself, and based on damned little data.

Without a leader, an agency staffed by people like us can deteriorate into knots of highly educated gossips, hassling over this, haggling over that, "processing" this feeling, "working through" that feeling, pondering the imponderable, sorting out the unsortable until, as sometimes happens, the better people get a bellyful of the bellyaching and lack of leadership and start looking for jobs in organizations that are not paralyzed by their own self-analysis.

If you have ever watched an entire agency put itself on the therapeutic couch and then invite its own staff in to conduct the cure, then I don't need to tell you what a grand case of malpractice this can be. Since there will be as many interpretations for what is wrong with the organizations as there are clinical staff, without a leader who can lead, the patient will likely perish.

In my view there should be both pride and privilege in what we do as managers and leaders; the pride comes from doing the hard things, the privilege is being asked to do them.

We should not work longer hours than our staff, except when the project must be completed. We should not take work home at night, except when the work must get done. We should not do for others, except when they cannot do for themselves. We should not make the impossible decisions, except when they must be made. We should not put our personal desires aside, except when our agency, our staff, and our clients require it of us. We should not take the painful actions, except when they must be taken.

If you believe in the mission of your agency, the purpose of your work as a manager and that you are, in the last analysis, a leader, then in time the difficult things will come easily. You will not think twice about a 7:00 A.M. breakfast meeting, an evening spent brainstorming some problem or other, or the worry time you put in about some troubled employee. You will move quickly and surely to deal with problems. And each time you push through some seemingly impossible task, you will come out of it a bit wiser, a bit more seasoned, and a bit stronger for having endured. And in the best of times, you will not only help your staff earn a living, but you will help them earn that living with pride.

For my part, I consider it a privilege to be asked to tackle the tough problems, and especially the nasty, impossible, complex, insoluble ones. Let other people handle the little problems— me, I want the big ones. The bigger the better. When someone comes to me with the most difficult, intransigent, miserable situation they have ever seen, I am positively delighted to be given a shot at trying to help him solve it.

In my own and entirely personal view, our work as leaders is a commitment, not a job; a career, not an assignment. For me the work has been a tremendous source of satisfaction and accomplishment without which my life as a clinician and psychologist might have been only good, instead of great. As adventures go, I can recommend no other more highly.

Bibliography

The following reference books are arranged by subject.

Behavioral Managment
Campbell, John P., Marvin D. Dunnette, Edward E. Lawler III, and Karl E. Weick, Jr. *Managerial Behavior, Performance, and Effectiveness.* New York: McGraw-Hill Book Company, 1970.

Miller, Lawrence E. *Behavior Management: The New Science of Managing People at Work.* New York: John Wiley & Sons, 1978.

Miller, Lawrence E. *Behavior Management: New Skills for Business and Industry.* Atlanta, Georgia: Behavioral Systems, Inc., 1974.

O'Brien, Richard M., Alyce M. Dickinson, and Michael P. Rosow. *Industrial Behavior Modification: A Management Handbook.* Elmsford, NY: Pergamon Press, 1982.

Management Theory and Practice
Drucker, Peter F. *Management: Tasks, Responsibilities, Practices.* New York: Harper & Row, 1973.

Herzberg, Frederick. *Work and the Nature of Man.* New York: World Publishing Company, 1966.

McGregor, Douglas. *The Human Side of Enterprise.* New York: McGraw-Hill Book Company, 1960.

Mali, Paul. *Managing by Objectives.* New York: Wiley-Interscience, 1972.

Mintzberg, Henry. *The Nature of Managerial Work.* New York: Harper & Row, 1973.

Morrisey, George S. *Management by Objectives and Results.* Reading, MA: Addison-Wesley, 1970.

Odiorne, George S. *Management by Objectives.* New York: Pittman Publishing Company, 1965.

Raia, Anthony P. *Managing by Objectives.* Glenview, IL: Scott Foresman & Company, 1974.

Management, Leadership, and Supervision

Bennis, Warren, and Burt Nanus. *Leaders: The Strategies for Taking Charge.* New York: Harper & Row, 1985.

Bothwell, Lin. *The Art of Leadership.* Englewood Cliffs, NJ: Prentice Hall, 1983.

Bruch, H. *Learning Psychotherapy: Rationale and Ground Rules.* Cambridge, MA: Harvard University Press, 1974.

Ekstein, R., and R. S. Wallerstein. *Teaching and Learning Psychotherapy.* New York: International Universities Press, 1972.

Fallon, William K., ed. *The AMA Management Handbook.* American Management Association, 1983.

Hess, Allen K., ed. *Psychotheraphy Supervision: Theory, Research, and Practice.* New York: John Wiley & Sons, Inc., 1980.

Josefowitz, Natasha, Ph.D. *You're the Boss.* New York: Warner Books, 1985.

Peters, Thomas J., and Robert H. Waterman, Jr. *In Search of Excellence.* New York: Warner Books, 1982.

Townsen, Robert. *Up the Organization.* New York: Fawcett Crest Books, 1970.

Vroom, Victor H., and Edward L. Dici, ed. *Management and Motivation.* New York: Penguin, 1983.

THE CONTINUUM
COUNSELING LIBRARY
Books of Related Interest

——Robert W. Buckingham
CARE OF THE DYING CHILD
A Practical Guide for Those Who Help Others
"Buckingham's book delivers a powerful, poignant message deserving a wide readership."—*Library Journal* $16.95

——Alastair V. Campbell, ed.
A DICTIONARY OF PASTORAL CARE
Provides information on the essentials of counseling and the kinds of problems encountered in pastoral practice. The approach is interdenominational and interdisciplinary. Contains over 300 entries by 185 authors in the fields of theology, philosophy, psychology, and sociology as well as from the theoretical background of psychotherapy and counseling. $24.50

——H.J. Eysenck, W. Arnold, and R. Meili, eds.
ENCYCLOPEDIA OF PSYCHOLOGY
Covering all aspects of psychology, this book features brief definitions and essays by subject specialists.
"An authoritative reference book in a clear and intelligible language. Essential."—*Booklist* $60.00

_____Lucy Freeman
FIGHT AGAINST FEARS
With a new Introduction by
Flora Rheta Schreiber
More than a million copies sold; the new—and only
available—edition of the first, and still best, true story of a
modern woman's journey of self-discovery through
psychoanalysis. $10.95

_____Lucy Freeman and Kerstin Kupfermann
THE POWER OF FANTASY
*Where Our Daydreams Come From, and How They Can Help or
Harm Us*
This is the first book to explain the role of both daydreams
and unconscious fantasies in our lives, helping us to
distinguish between those that can unleash our creativity and
those that can emotionally cripple us. $16.95

_____Marion Howard
HOW TO HELP YOUR TEENAGER
POSTPONE SEXUAL INVOLVEMENT
Based on a national educational program that works, this
book advises parents, teachers, and counselors on how they
can help their teens resist social and peer pressures
regarding sex. $14.95

_____Marion Howard
SOMETIMES I WONDER ABOUT ME
Teenagers and Mental Health
Combines fictional narratives with sound, understandable
professional advice to help teenagers recognize the
difference between serious problems and normal problems
of adjustment. $9.95

_____Janice N. McLean and Sheila A. Knights
PHOBICS AND OTHER PANIC VICTIMS
A Practical Guide for Those Who Help Them
"A must for the phobic, spouse and family, and for the
physician and support people who help them. It can spell
the difference between partial therapy with partial results
and comprehensive therapy and recovery."—Arthur B.
Hardy, M.D., Founder, TERRAP Phobia Program, and Past
President, Phobia Society of America **$15.95**

_____Cherry Boone O'Neill
DEAR CHERRY
Questions and Answers on Eating Disorders
Practical and inspiring advice on eating disorders from the
best-selling author of *Starving for Attention.* **$8.95**

_____Paul G. Quinnett
**ON BECOMING A HEALTH
AND HUMAN SERVICES MANAGER**
A Practical Guide for Clinicians and Counselors
A new and essential guide to management for everyone in
the helping professions—from mental health to nursing,
from social work to teaching. **$17.95**

_____Paul G. Quinnett
SUICIDE: THE FOREVER DECISION
*For Those Thinking About Suicide,
and for Those Who Know, Love, or Counsel Them*
"A treasure—this book can help save lives. It will be
especially valuable not only to those who are thinking about
suicide but to such nonprofessional counselors as teachers,
clergy, doctors, nurses, and to experienced therapists."—
William Van Ornum, psychotherapist and author
$18.95 hc $7.95 pbk

————Paul G. Quinnett
THE TROUBLED PEOPLE BOOK
A practical and positive guide to the world of psychotherapy
and psychotherapists. "Without a doubt one of the most
honest, reassuring, nonpaternalistic, and useful self-help
books ever to appear."—*Booklist* $9.95

————Judah L. Ronch
ALZHEIMER'S DISEASE
A Practical Guide for Those Who Help Others
Must reading for everyone—from family members to
professional caregivers—who must deal with the effects of
this tragic disease on a daily basis. Filled with illustrative
examples as well as facts, this book provides sensitive insights
into dealing with one's feelings as well as with such practical
advice as how to choose long-term care. $15.95

————John R. Shack
COUPLES COUNSELING
A Practical Guide for Those Who Help Others
An essential guide to dealing with the 20 percent of all
counseling situations that involve the relationship of two
people. $15.95

————Stuart Sutherland
**THE INTERNATIONAL DICTIONARY OF
PSYCHOLOGY**
This new dictionary of psychology also covers a wide range
of related disciplines, from anthropology to
sociology. $49.95

_____Joan Leslie Taylor
IN THE LIGHT OF DYING
The Journals of a Hospice Volunteer
A rare and beautiful book about death and dying that
affirms life and will inspire an attitude of love. "Beautifully
recounts the healing (our own) that results from service to
others, and might well be considered as required reading for
hospice volunteers."—Stephen Levine $17.95

_____Montague Ullman, M.D. and Claire Limmer, M.S., eds.
THE VARIETY OF DREAM EXPERIENCE
Expanding Our Ways of Working With Dreams
"Lucidly describes the beneficial impact dream analysis can
have in diverse fields and in society as a whole. An erudite,
illuminating investigation."—*Booklist* $19.95 hc $11.95 pbk

_____William Van Ornum and John Mordock
CRISIS COUNSELING WITH CHILDREN AND
ADOLESCENTS
"It's the kind of book every parent should keep on the shelf
next to nutrition, medical, and Dr. Spock books."—*Marriage
& Family Living* $9.95

_____William Van Ornum and Mary W. Van Ornum
TALKING TO CHILDREN ABOUT NUCLEAR WAR
"A wise book. A needed book. An urgent book."
—Dr. Karl A. Menninger $15.95 hc $7.95 pbk

At your bookstore, or to order directly, send your check or
money order (adding $2.00 extra per book for postage and
handling, up to $5.00 maximum) to:

The Continuum Publishing Company
370 Lexington Avenue
New York, NY 10017